$ 1.50

Italian for the Opera

Robert Stuart Thomson

Godwin Books, Vancouver.

Italian for the Opera
Copyright © 1992 by Robert Stuart Thomson
Printed by Friesen Press, Manitoba, Canada

Set in 11/13 point Times (Lasercomp)
by Synchronoptical Typesetting Services,
2164 Wall Street, Vancouver, BC

Although efforts have been made to trace
the present copyright holders of photographs, the publishers apologize in advance
for any unintentional omission or neglect
and will be pleased to insert the appropriate acknowledgement to companies or in-
dividuals in any subsequent edition of this
book.

ISBN 0-9696774-0-5

Printed in Canada

TABLE OF CONTENTS

"The libretto, then, is the thing. For these operas are really great poetry in words and music. The words must be read and known; they constitute the form, the structure. The music is the color whose magnificence is not fully realized until it is made glorious and brilliant in the light of the underlying poetry."

From the Forward to "The Authentic Librettos of the Wagner Operas".

PREFACE

Who would have thought that in the 1990's opera would be gaining in popularity? Yet it is so. In spite of this popularity, however, no guide is currently available for those who would like to learn the Italian of the opera. This is somewhat odd, when you consider that there are plenty of books available on modern Italian grammar and Italian for tourists (neither of which will help you much when it comes to opera) and that opera and opera lovers have been around for a long time. The lack of a good guide is especially lamentable for serious students of voice, etc., who would benefit a great deal if they could understand the libretto in depth.

This book aims to fill the gap. Its purpose is **not** to explore in long-winded depth every aspect of libretto Italian, but rather to present in clear, jargon-free language and logical steps a most important key to the operatic world of Mozart, Rossini, Bellini, Verdi, Puccini, etc. You don't have to be a linguistic whiz or a native Italian. All it takes is some pleasurable application. As for the native Italian reader, you too might find this book of interest, especially if you find the words and pattern of "La vecchia lingua" difficult.

For most people, grammar is an unpleasant word which conjures up images of boredom and picky pedantry. Used carefully, however, grammar is illuminating, even fun, and that is the impression I hope that you will have when you have read this book.

As with most languages, verbs are the key to quick success and for this reason a large chunk of the book is devoted to them. Every effort has been made not to belabor the obvious and to devote ample time to the more demanding points like the subjunctive (which is really not **that** difficult!), the dative of advantage, and the like.

By the end of the book you should understand operatic Italian well enough to make your way through most parts of most librettos, which is no mean achievement.

"Italian for the Opera" draws on hundreds of interesting quotations from famous operas and whenever possible I have tried to use extracts from well-known arias. In the pages which follow you will also find interesting anecdotes, illustrations and even self-testing exercises (with answer keys at the back of the book) should you wish to monitor your progress. Comments on the significance of the libretto i. e. how understanding it adds to your appreciation, have been included as well. It is a truism but nonetheless worth repeating: only by understanding the original libretto will you sound the bottom of opera's depths.

In brief, whether you are an enthusiastic beginner, a serious student of opera, or an established aficionado I think that you will enjoy this trip through the magical and yet so human world of the Italian opera libretto.

The author wishes to thank the following for their encouragement:

Dr. Alan Aberbach, Dr. Leland Fox, Dr. Walter Lippincott Jr., Dr. Charles Mackie, Dr. Richard Sjoerdsma, Dr. French Tickner.

ITALIAN FOR THE OPERA

CHAPTER ONE

This is a book for those opera lovers who are willing to accept the challenge of learning the Italian of the opera. As most readers already know, operatic Italian is not what you hear when you de-plane at Leonardo da Vinci airport (although Italians being what they are, it would not be surprising to hear someone singing an aria...). The mainstream of operatic Italian comes to us through the influence of one composer: Pietro Metastasio (1698-1782). Metas-tasio's librettos set the tone for just about everything to follow (Mozart, Rossini, Bellini, Donizetti, Verdi, Puccini, etc.)

Metastasio's Italian has its own peculiar charm. It is highly literary and sometimes diabolically difficult: terse, twisted, bristling with Latinisms and many rare, antiquated expressions. And yet the fact remains that the idiom which Metastasio popularized cannot be simplified. It might as well be engraved in bronze. The opera lover must accept that Metastasio's Italian, like Popeye, "is what it is" and takes time to master.

The purpose of this book is to present Metastasio's Italian -- the Italian of the opera -- as clearly and efficiently as possible. With a small time investment you can crack Metastasio's code and master his idiom. Some knowledge of French and/or Italian/Spanish would help. So would an acquaintance with Latin, but such knowledge is not necessary. Whatever your background, this book is designed to help you to focus on operatic Italian without having the problem aggravated by having to learn modern spoken Italian as well.

NOTE: THE NEXT 8 PAGES DEAL WITH COMPLEX BACKGROUND ISSUES. IF YOU ARE NOT FAMILIAR WITH ITALIAN SKIP TO P. 9 AND COME BACK TO PP. 2-8 WHEN YOU HAVE READ THE REST OF THE BOOK.

Although operatic and modern Italian coincide to some degree, there are many differences, and it is most efficient to learn them separately (and not simultaneously, as I tried to do as a student in Florence in 1960.) An advantage to studying operatic Italian on its own is that you can focus on the difficulties which are peculiar to it. If you study **Rigoletto**, for instance, you will find that there are only nine verb tenses to learn. If you study modern Italian on its own with a view to understanding opera, you will be thwarted by several problems: more than twenty verb tenses and a huge, often irrelevant vocabulary, not to mention the fact that no book about modern Italian will deal with opera's own obsolete language. For maximum focus, there is much to be said for studying operatic Italian on its own.

At the same time, since there is some overlapping (especially grammatically) between operatic Italian and modern Italian, much of what you learn in this book will serve you well when travelling in Italy. It will also serve you well if you ever decide to read the great Italian classics -- Dante, Petrarch and Boccaccio -- who were around centuries before opera was invented and profoundly influenced almost every Italian writer (incl. the librettists) in their wake.[1]

*"Dr. Alfred Alexander, a Harley Street specialist, found in a study on operatic comprehension that the average unprepared Italian listening to **Rigoletto** will understand only about 15% of the libretto. He also found that reading the libretto attentively just once doubles or trebles the number of words that can be understood." (Quoted from an article by Stephen Fay which appeared in **The Sunday Times** on April 25, 1982.) Dr. Alexander's findings perhaps can be taken with a grain of salt (Where did he find "average Italians"? How on earth could he*

[1] e. g., when Violetta in **La Traviata** says, "O gioia ch'io non conobbi/Esser' amata amando." (Oh joy I have not known/To be loved while loving in turn.) there is a strong echo of Dante's Francesca da Rimini's "Amor, ch'a nullo amato amar' perdona." Such echoes abound in opera.

test such a complex -- even untestable? -- subject and obtain such precise results? etc.) but he does raise interesting questions. The "bottom line" is this: do you have to almost memorize a libretto in order to really understand an opera?

By working your way through this book you will reap many rewards. No longer will you have to endure the inaccuracy and stiltedness of an English translation; you will have accurate first-hand knowledge of what is being said in the opera and because of this you will begin to **feel opera** the way a knowledgeable Italian feels it.[2] The complete operatic experience is ready to unfold before you: plot, character, dialogue, symbolism, connotation, irony, humor, innuendo, and literary echoes. Your grasp of the customs and the social/historical background will also acquire a new dimension. Hitherto untranslatable expressions will come to you with **full direct impact**. So will puns and allusions. Not least of the benefits to be gained will be the sheer sensual pleasure of the Italian -- its amazing sonority and musicality. When the Duke in **Rigoletto** sings "Stanco son' io!" (I am tired!) there is a voluptuousness and languor in the very sounds of the words which "I am tired." (or "Je suis fatigué." or "Ich bin müde." or "Estoy cansado." can't possibly convey.

What I have written above will be clearer if we take a close look at two extracts (from **Rigoletto**) and ask these questions: How does operatic Italian differ from modern Italian? How do (all) translations misrepresent the original? What are some of the distinctive aspects of operatic Italian? Below I have written four versions of the same extract: (1) the original libretto; (2) a translation into modern Italian;

---

[2] An example is when the Courtiers laugh about Rigoletto's being left "scornato ad imprecar'" (Act II). This has been translated as "scorned and cursing" but such a translation does nothing to convey the glaring connotation/association of "cornuto" i. e. cuckolded, which is implicit only in the original. An element of cruel humour (very much a part of Rigoletto and his world) is therefore lost in the translation.

(3) a literal, accurate English translation; and (4) the kind of "bowdlerized" English translation which often comes with your C.D.'s or L. P.'s. In **La Donna è Mobile** the Duke sings the following lines:

> Pur' mai non sentesi
> Felice appieno
> Chi su quel seno
> Non liba amore.

In modern Italian it would go as follows, which, as you can see, is just different enough to cause problems:

> Eppure colui che
> Non beve amore su quel seno
> Non si sente mai
> Completement felice.

In an accurate, literal translation the meaning is as follows:

> And yet whoever
> does not drink love on that breast
> Never feels completely happy.

Note that a literal translation is accurate but often very stilted, which is one of the reasons why most translators take liberty in their translations. Unfortunately, all too often this liberty crosses the boundary into inaccuracy and, even worse, totally misleading versions. Take, for example, the following bowdlerized translation which, unfortunately, is not that uncommon:

> Yet the man never knows
> Complete happiness
> Who does not taste
> Love in her arms.

You can see from this comparison the value of learning the original. It is much better (more vivid, more colorful, more complex, more violent, etc.) than any of the translations and cannot be accurately conveyed by any of them. Let's have another look at these lines and note how they differ from the Bowdlerized version.

> Pur **mai** non s<u>e</u>ntesi
> Yet never feels
> Felice appieno
> Completely happy
> Chi su quel **seno**
> He (who) on that breast
> Non **liba amore.**
> Does not drink love.

(1) Only the original version ("Pur' mai non s<u>e</u>ntesi...") rhymes and flows. In comparison the English is stilted and prosaic.
(2) Placed at the beginning of the sentence "mai" has much greater impact than "never"
(3) "S<u>e</u>ntesi" (from 'sentire', to feel), conveys a sensual dimension which is missing in "knows".
(4) "seno" (breast) conveys much more sensuality and eroticism than "arms" (Such a euphemistic cliché!).
(5) By being placed at the end of the verse, "amore" is much more forceful than "love".
(6) "Liba" (from 'libare', to drink, to drink a toast to) has aristocratic, hedonistic, even pagan (a "libation to the Gods", etc.) connotations which are almost (?) impossible to translate effectively.

In short, the sensuality and eroticism of the original Italian succeeds far better than the English translation in conveying the sensual, libertine character of the Duke as well as his paradoxical nature (i. e. the interesting combination of cynicism and idealism), not to mention the themes of sexual love, obsession, revenge, abduction, sycophancy, self-sacrifice, etc., which are so richly developed in **Rigoletto.** As you master operatic Italian you will discover many such riches in the original libretto. It is well worth the effort.[3]

[3] See page six for the footnote.

Before discussing the stress pattern and sounds of Italian it will help if you bear in mind some of the typical peculiarities of operatic Italian. The opening lines of **Rigoletto** will show you what I mean:

DUKE   1   Della mia bella incognita borghese
                (Of my beautiful unknown townswoman)
          2   Toccare il fin' dell'avventura io voglio.
                (Attain the objective of the affair I want to.)
BORSA   3   Di quella giovin' che vedete al tempio?
                (Of that girl whom you see at the temple?)
DUKE   4   Da tre mesi ogni festa.
                (For three months now every holy day.)
BORSA   5   La sua dimora?
                (Her dwelling?)

You can see four characteristic things about operatic Italian in these lines:

1. opera tends to favor rare, unusual and often obsolete words. Latinisms, fourteenth century expressions, borrowings from French -- all are common currency. In the passage above, "incognita" (unknown) in line one is a Latinism and is preferred to the more common "sconosciuta". In line three "tempio" is now obsolete in the sense used; "chiesa" would be the usual word. In line five "dimora" is a borrowing from the French, the more usual word being "casa". In **Lucia di Lammermoor** the wedding is referred to as a "prosapia", which you could say is much more Latin than Italian (the modern Italian would be "matrimonio" or "sposalizio").

---

[3] When you understand the original libretto it is amusing to pick out the errors. In one version of **Il Barbiere**, for instance, you find the following misleading versions: "Voglio ammazzare!" (Literally, "I want to murder.") rendered as "Let me get at him!" (The Count); "Eh, non son' matto!" (Literally, "Hey, I'm not crazy!") translated as "Trust me, sir." (Figaro); and "Ma che tutti sian' d'accordo!" (Literally, "But would that all could agree!") twisted into "Well, at any rate they are all in agreement." (!) (Basilio).

2. opera likes to shorten words. In line two "il fin'" (the objective) is short for "il fine". In line three "giovin'" (young girl/youth) is short for "giovine".
3. opera often prefers a twisted, unnatural word order reminiscent of Latin. The first two lines of the **Rigoletto** extract above are typical. The following would be the normal word order:

> "Io voglio toccare il fin' dell'avventura della mia bella
> I want attain   the objective of the affair with my beautiful
> incognita borghese."
> unknown townswoman.

In comparison, notice how contorted are the lines of the original libretto. Another line, this time from **Aïda**, shows the same tendency:

> "Speme non v'ha pel mio dolor'" (original, in the libretto)
> Non v'ha speme pel mio dolor'. (normal word order)
> Non c'è speranza per il mio dolore. (modern Italian)
> There is no hope for my grief. (translation)

In opera, sentences can be twisted any number of ways and this twisted word order, along with the specialized vocabulary, constitute the two biggest difficulties. There is often a good reason for the twisted word order, of course, i. e. the specific musical needs of the composer. If the composer creates just the right musical phrase, surely the librettist is going to have to juggle words to accommodate him, and not vice versa. Besides, many of these librettists were excellent Latinists and were fond of twisting Italian around in very Latinate ways. (A sentence in Latin can be written in just about any word order you like because the 'case endings' will make the relationships between the various parts of the sentence very clear.) However, whatever the reasons for operatic Italian's word order, it certainly doesn't make it any easier. On the contrary. Nevertheless, this elasticity has its purpose, giving the composer and librettist much scope in meter and rhyme, especially in the use of dramatic emphasis, e. g. the periodic sentence (in which the strongest word is not revealed until the very end of the sentence, where it hits with maximal power: "Degli Egizi tu sei la schiava!" (Of the Egyptians you are the slave! -- Amneris to Aïda). Without such inversions opera would lose much of its variety and dramatic impact.

4. Operatic Italian likes to say much in few words. This concision is evident in both the above passages. Verdi himself commented on the importance of concision in a letter to his great (yet so modest) librettist, Piave:

> *Dear Piave,*
> *I have received your verses (to **La Forza del Destino**)*
> *and, if I may say so, I don't like them. You talk to*
> *me about 100 syllables!! And it's obvious that 100*
> *syllables aren't enough when you take 25 to say the*
> *sun is setting!!! The line 'Duopo e (sic) sia l'opra*
> *truce compita' is too hard, and even worse is 'Un*
> *Requiem, un Pater...e tutto ha fin''.(...)*
> *Then, the seven-syllabled lines!!! For the love of*
> *God, don't end lines with 'che', 'piu' (sic) and 'an-*
> *cor'.*
> *Now then, can't you do better, retaining as far as*
> *possible the words I sent you, but turning them into*
> *better rhymes?*
> *(Written on December 20, 1864. Quoted from p. 135*
> *of Osborne's **Letters of Giuseppe Verdi**).*

There are a few other peculiarities as well, notably pleonasms (superfluous words) and elipses (omitted words) to watch for in librettos, but these will be discussed later (pp. 46, 129). With these general points in mind let us now look at the essential elements of Italian pronunciation.

CHAPTER TWO

ITALIAN PRONUNCIATION

THE STRESS PATTERN AND SOUNDS OF ITALIAN

The best way to learn the sounds of Italian is to listen carefully to native speakers on a good sound system. Although some non-natives have acquired a very good accent, even the best of these is not always reliable and the worst (including some very popular and famous singers) do not have very good accents at all. One of the rather ironic benefits of learning operatic Italian is that you will be able to detect faults (in pronunciation and in some editions of the libretto itself) where you previously detected none. (In some cases the amazing clarity of compact discs has had a similar effect, revealing defects where none were discernible before.)

There are two main aspects to the pronunciation of Italian: stress and sound quality. The following pages will explain the essentials.

A. THE STRESS PATTERN OF OPERATIC ITALIAN

While working your way through this book you will need to bear in mind the question of stress i. e. where each syllable is accented. Like English, Italian is a highly stressed language, which gives it a varied rhythm pattern and a very melodious, sing-song quality (which the Italians call "cantilena").[4] Although there is a normal stress pattern in Italian (words are usually accented on the second to the last syllable, e. g., "la forza del destino"), **it is often impossible to predict where the stress will fall in an Italian word,** which makes Italian very difficult, even as difficult as English in this respect. Many words simply have to be learned on their own.

---

[4] A good example of 'cantilena' in an opera would be Lady Macbeth reading the letter from her husband in Verdi's **Macbeth** or Violetta reading Giorgio Germont's letter in **La Traviata**.

Unfortunately, there are no accent marks to help you (as there are, say, in Spanish, where the acute accent is regularly used to mark exceptions to the stress rule) with the irregularities. Nor is there a predictable rhythm pattern, as there is in French (and this it is which makes Italian difficult for them too!)

Because stress is such a problem, throughout this book I have underlined **the vowel of the stressed syllable** in any words of un-predictable stress. Examples:

al solito   (usually)
il brindisi (the toast)
colpevole (guilty)
indagini   (investigations)
indomito (unconquered)
il patibolo(the hangman's
                    /scaffold)

qualsiasi (any, whatsoever)
la smania (the craze, passion,
                    /strange obsession)
la tenebra (the shadow)
il vindice (the avenger)
i vortici (the eddies)

Most of the words which I have underlined take the accent on the third to the last syllable, which the Italians picturesquely call the "accento sdrucciolo" (literally, "the slippery accent"). Such words constitute a huge (and unpredictable) group in Italian. One of the few places where you can actually count on finding them is in the third person plural of most verb tenses: "apparvero" (they appeared), "furono" (they went), "temono" (they fear), "vengono" (they are coming), etc.

When the stress falls on the last syllable, it is always marked for you with a grave (\) accent:

l'amistà (friendship)
ciò (that—pronoun)
condannò (he/she
                    /condemned)
già (already)
Gualtier Maldè
lassù (up there)

osò (he/she dared)
parlerò (I will speak)
perchè (because; why)
più (more, any longer)
potè (he/she could)
potrà (he/she will be able)
pregherà (he/she will pray)
Radamès

Some one syllable words carry a grave accent to distinguish them from 'look-alikes':

da (from—preposition)	is not to be confused with dà (he/she gives—verb)
di (of—preposition)	is not to be confused with dì (il dì—noun).
la (the—article)	is not to be confused with là (there—adverb).
ne (of it, by us, etc. —pronoun)	is not to be confused with nè (neither—conjunction).

(However, you don't need to worry about these distinctions because if you work your way carefully through this book you will understand the function of every word in every sentence and can't possibly be fooled.) The grave accent is by far the most common accent in Italian and the only important one. Note that it usually marks only stress and not, as does its French look-alike, the sound quality of the vowel.

The stress pattern of Italian is a major difficulty, then, and in opera this problem is aggravated by the demands of musical phrasing i. e. sometimes **the sequence of notes demands incorrect stress** and to sing the notes correctly **you have to stress words the wrong way**. A kind of poetic licence has to be taken in verses like these:

(1) "Egli è mestiere che tu subito cada." (Tosca to Mario)
It is necessary that you fall right away.
To sing it correctly you must accentuate the "bi" in **subito**.
(2) "(...) ch'io ti lasci fuggir' mai!" (Don. Elvira to Don Giov.)
...that I ever let you flee!
In singing this phrase you have to stress the "fug" in **fuggir'**
Otherwise it doesn't work.
(3) "(...) se il mio sogno s'avverasse!" (Radamès in 'Celeste Aïda').
... if only my dream were to come true! Singing demands that you incorrectly accent the "av" in **avverasse**.

(4) "(...) mangiar' mal' e mal' dormir'!" to eat badly and sleep badly. (Leporello in Don Giovanni). Sung correctly, the first "a" in 'mangiar'' is stressed, even if it is incorrect.

The questions of whether Italian operas should be presented in translation, whether a detailed understanding of the libretto is really worth the effort, and the like, have always been controversial. Travelling around Northern Italy in the early 1800's, Stendhal noted amongst even his Italian hosts some very cavalier attitudes towards librettos: "Still more apprehensive of the disagreeable impression which might be gleaned from the libretto, Signora B***, in Venice, used to refuse to allow anybody at all to bring it into her box, even at the premiere. She used to get someone to prepare her a summary of the plot, some forty lines in all; and then, during the performance, she would be informed, in four or five words, of the theme of each aria (...) for instance, (...) Lindoro is passionately in love; Isabella is flirting with the Bey, etc. (...) In such a fashion should all libretti be printed for those (...) who appreciate music as music is appreciated in Venice." (from Stendhal's 'Life of Rossini'). Incredibly, as great an opera enthusiast as Stendhal seems to have held views similar to those of the Signora B***. Perhaps neither would have reacted to librettos this way had he/she been born forty years later, in time to feel the verbal power of **Rigoletto**. *On the other hand, perhaps it's an incurable form of anti-intellectual snobbery based on an avoidance of making the effort required to come to terms with the libretto. Certainly this kind of reaction is still very much with us and even today it is not uncommon to hear otherwise intelligent, sensitive people contend that the* **truly musical** *person does not need to understand the libretto! One hears similar nonsense about* *people with 'natural rhythm' not needing to study ballroom dancing. (Note : **I have inserted quotations from time to time in order to raise, and perhaps answer, some questions.**)*

B. THE SOUNDS OF OPERATIC ITALIAN

As pure and musical as Italian is, pronouncing the language correctly is far from simple and can only be learned by listening carefully to a great deal of Italian. This being the case, what follows is only a summary of the main points but it should be enough.

VOWELS

These are the same as in English, except that Italian has no "y". Also, the Italian vowels have a purer sound. As for the details, Italian distinguishes between a "close" [o] (the 'o' of the English 'hotel') e. g., "il dono" (the gift) and an "open" [ɔ] (as in the English 'odd') e. g., "la donna". Similarly, the "close" [e] (the sound of the English 'date') e. g., "felice" (happy) is quite different from the "open" [ɛ] (the 'e' of the English 'Edward') e. g., "Edgardo". This close (long) and open (short) vowels business is complex and can be mastered only through lengthy exposure to the language. Some Italian dictionaries will help you to sort it out because they use the International Phonetic Alphabet (IPA) in which an [o] indicates a close 'o' and an [ɔ] indicates an open 'o'. They also use an [e] for a close 'e' and a [ɛ] for an open 'e'.

Diphthongs (two vowels coming together—io, ia, ei, ai, au and the like—) are difficult and unpredictable. "Ei" (short for "egli", i. e. 'he' in English) is pronounced like "aye—ee", in two syllables, with the accent on the "e". "Possiede", (from the infinitive 'possedere', meaning 'he/she possesses') is pronounced "poh-see-aye-day", with the accent on the "e". "Potria" (I could, he could) is pronounced "poh-tree-uh", with the accent unmistakably on the "i".

13

To complicate matters, you do encounter triphthongs: "la gioia", 'joy' in English ("la joy yuh") and others, most of which can only be learned by listening, e. g., "il giuoco" (the game), "miei" ('my', masculine plural adjective), and "muoia" ("Let him die!", present subjunctive of 'morire', to die). The ultimate tester has to be "la ghiacciaia", the ice-box, which is used by Marcello to describe Musetta's coquettish heart in **La Bohème.** Although I have underlined a stressed syllable in each of these words, it is only an approximation; the only way to learn them is by listening. How could you guess that "già" (sounds like Jack) is only one syllable?

CONSONANTS

The good news is that in Italian there is no J, K, W or X. Having said that, the following are the main points to remember about consonants.

Most important: double consonants like "bb", "gg", "mm" are pronounced in such a way that you linger on each of the two consonants: "Mamma, quel vino è generoso...", "Mio caro babbo...", "la fiamma dell'amore"...

"C"	is hard (as in the English 'coat') before a, o, and u: "castello".
"C"	is soft (as in the English 'church') before e and i: "C'è" ('there is').
"CH"	is hard: "che" ('what', 'which').
"G"	is hard (as in the English 'good') before a, o, and u: "gobbo (hunchback)
"G"	is soft (as in the English 'gem') before e and i: "gemma" ('gem').
"GH"	is hard: "ghiaccio" ('ice').
"GL"	has no equivalent in English. "Egli" ('He'). It sounds a bit like the 'lli' part of the English word 'million'.
"GN"	before a vowel also has no English equivalent e. g., "ignoro" ('I don't know.') It resembles the 'ni' part of the English word 'onion'.

14

"H"	is silent: "Ho" ('I have').
"QU"	is like the "qu" in the English "queen": "questa" ('this one').
"S"	is usually like the "s" of the English "snake": "salvare" ('to save').
"S"	between vowels is pronounced like a "z": "casa" ('house'). Contrast Spanish.
"SC"	is soft (like the English word 'shoe') before e and i: "scellerato" ('rascal', 'wretch', 'rat').
"SCH"	is hard (like the English 'skipper'): "scherzi" (you're joking).
"Z"	can be like the English "ts" in "its": "vil(e) razza dannata" ('damned vile race').

With this look at the background you are now ready to study operatic Italian in depth. A logical and understandable approach is based on parts of speech. This is the basis of the method which follows and in spite of that dreaded phrase "parts of speech" I think you will find it interesting. Cari lettori miei, andate pure avanti! But first, two little anecdotes (both attributed to Mr. Shaw).

—*"Can you speak Italian, Mr. (George Bernard) Shaw?"*
—*"Well, I can order a bowl of poison and a dagger, but I can't order a glass of milk."*

"I know about twenty words of operatic Italian, available perhaps for making love or expressing murderous jealousy but totally useless for reasonable human intercourse."

CHAPTER THREE

THE METHOD BEHIND
"ITALIAN FOR THE OPERA"

Operatic Italian is difficult but with a good method you can learn it fairly quickly. "Italian for the Opera" is based on three main ideas:

(1) learning to recognize parts of speech is a great shortcut;
(2) verbs are the most important part of speech;
(3) librettists favour certain peculiar expressions which constantly crop up (datives of advantage, inversions, and "demon words" like 'pure').

If you can recognize these, you have a big advantage. By doing the exercises at the end of each section then checking your answers in Chapter Twelve you can monitor your progress. If you want to delve further, try working your way through one of the Verdi librettos in Mr. Weaver's very accurate book (see my bibliography) **while listening to a recording of the same opera.** In this way you will master the vocabulary, the structures and the pronunciation.

PARTS OF SPEECH

Some readers might come close to cardiac arrest at the very mention of "parts of speech". Not to worry! They can be approached without pedantry. Parts of speech are really very easy and a knowledge of them enables you to divide and conquer the libretto. There are only nine parts of speech in all: (1) noun; (2) article; (3) preposition; (4) adjective; (5) adverb; (6) pronoun; (7) conjunction; (8) interjection; and (9) verb. This is the order in which they will be discussed. A glance at the Table of Contents will show you how relatively easy all of them (except the verbs!) are.

OUTLINE OF THE NINE PARTS OF SPEECH
WITH EXAMPLES

NAME WHAT IT DOES	EXAMPLES

1. NOUN Names a person, place or thing.

Aïda, Parigi (Paris), il cielo (sky; heaven).

"Ridi   del **duol'** che t'avvelena il **cuor'**!"
Laugh (for) the grief which poisons your heart!
(Canio in **I Pagliacci**).

2. ARTICLE
Goes with a noun.

uno, una, un' (a/an); il, lo, l', gli, la, l', le (the).

3. PREPOSITION
Connects nouns and pronouns to other words. Often shows space and time relationships.

di (of); a (to, in); in (in); su (on); da (from); prima di (before).

"Cercar', che giova? Al buio   non si trova!"
To search, what good In the dark it can't be found!
/does it do? (Rodolfo in **La Bohème**).

4. ADJECTIVE
Describes a noun or a pronoun.

cupo (dark, menacing); reo (evil); matto(crazy); tremendo (awesome and horrible).

"**Misera** Leonora, tremi!"
Wretched Leonora, tremble!
(Leonora to herself in **Il Trovatore**).

17

5. ADVERB

Tells how something
is done, or how often.

dolcemente (sweetly);
male (badly); assai (very)

"Non feci **mai**   male   ad <u>a</u>nima   viva!"
I **never** did   evil   to (a) soul   alive!
(Tosca in **Tosca**)

6. PRONOUN

Replaces nouns
(things or people).

io (I); <u>e</u>i (he); essa (she);
noi (we); me (me); etc.

"Ed **<u>e</u>i**   con   vere   l<u>a</u>crime   scrisse..."
And **he**   with   real   tears   wrote...
(The Prologue in **I Pagliacci**)

7. CONJUNCTION

Links chunks of a
sentence together.

e (and); però (but; therefore); perchè (because).

"**Poichè** in iscena anc<u>o</u>r' le antiche m<u>a</u>schere mette l'autore..."
Since   (on stage) again   the ancient masks   puts the author
Since the author puts the ancient masks on stage again.
(The Prologue to **I Pagliacci**).

8. INTERJECTION

Shows a sudden emotion.

"Tu taci, **ohimè!**"
You are silent, alas!
(Rigoletto to Marullo).
"Deh!" (I prithee).

9. VERB

Tells what is being done,
has been done, etc.
(action verbs).
Also can convey that
something is, was, will
be, etc. (linking verbs).

Io **tremo** (I tremble).
Voi congiuraste (You plotted)
"Ed **olezzava** la terra..."
(And the earth gave off a
fragrance..) From **Tosca**.
"Quel cor' chiuso <u>è</u> a me!"
That heart is closed to me!
(King Philip in **Don Carlo**)

18

Some of the famous blunders in opera resulted from a singer's poor grasp of the libretto. Vickers in "Great Opera Disasters" tells an amusing story: "A terrified new Don Giovanni walked on stage and began 'Il Mio Tesoro' instead of 'Dalla sua Pace'. It is said that the orchestra had such mastery of the score that as one man they instantaneously cut to the correct bar a hundred-odd pages later, with such aplomb that the audience assumed that for some reason the arias had been deliberately reversed..."

Before dealing systematically with the nine parts of speech (p. 24 ff.) let's identify them in two famous passages.

SKIPPING TO PAGE 21 IS OPTIONAL. YOU MIGHT PREFER TO COME BACK TO THESE PAGES WHEN YOU'VE FINISHED THE BOOK.

1. La   donna è   mobile
   ('A')   lady   is   changeable (i.e. untrustworthy)
   ART.   NOUN VERB ADJECTIVE
   ("La" doesn't mean "a", as I've translated, but sometimes a literal translation makes no sense. When I deliberately take such liberties, I will put the mistranslation in **inverted commas**.)

2. Qual'   piuma   al   vento.
   Like (a) feather   'in' the   wind.
   PREPOS. NOUN   PREP./ARTICLE NOUN

3. (Essa)   muta   d'accento
   (She)   changes accent (metaphor for speech)
   (PRONOUN VERB PREPOSITION/NOUN
   IS UNDERSTOOD)

4. E   di   pensiero.
And   (of)   thought. (i.e. she constantly
CONJUNC. PREP.   NOUN   changes her mind).

5. (È/è)   sempre   un amabile, leggiadro   viso: (ma)
(It is)   always   a loveable, beautiful   face: (but)
VERB   ADV'B   ART./ADJ. ADJECT.   NOUN   CONJ.

6. In   pianto   o   in   riso
In   tear(s)   or   in   laughter
PREP.   NOUN   CONJ.   PREP.   NOUN

7. E (è)   menzognero.
(It i. e.   her face   is 'apt to lie'.
VERB   ADJECTIVE

By closely examining the original Italian we get a much better sense of this celebrated passage: A woman is changeable and untrustworthy, like a feather in the wind. She changes her words and thoughts at a whim. Always a loveable, beautiful face (but) whether crying or laughing it is a false one. Note that the complexity derives from both the omitted words i. e. terseness (verses 3, 7) and from the subtle connotation of the original Italian. For these reasons a libretto yields its deepest secrets only if studied in the original. Only by grasping these linguistic subtleties is one likely to bridge the gap and appreciate the deeper thematic aspects i. e. the splendid irony of the passage is that the Duke himself is the most changeable, fickle fellow imaginable! Moreover, the two women whom we observe in his life, Gilda (a virgin) and Maddalena (a prostitute), seem to be totally reliable and devoted to him. Psychologically, Verdi, Piave, and Victor Hugo have created a masterful portrait of narcissistic projection.

Note the four characteristic features of operatic Italian mentioned earlier (pp. 6,7):

(1) **literary language**—"mobile", verse one; "viso", verse five; "menzognero", verse seven. ("Qual'", verse two, is peculiar to operatic Italian; in modern Italian it would be "come".) The feather as a metaphor for unpredictability is also typical of operatic Italian.

(2) **shortened words** (e. g., "qual'").

(3) **unusual word order** (Note the periodic: "Sempre un amabile...è menzognero." i.e. the meaning is clarified only with the last two words of the sentence.)

(4) **concision**. Notice how many words it takes to paraphrase the original! Certain words are omitted: the subject of "muta" is understood; an "è" (it is) is implied just before "sempre" and a "ma" (but) implied just after "viso". A remarkable richness of meaning is crammed into seven short verses.

> *"Everyone in Venice took up the aria, words and all. One heard it in **campo** and **calle**, on the bridges and in the gondolas, from Cannaregio to San Pietro di Castello. (...) Piave found the tune useful one day when he spotted a woman he had loved and lost approaching in the street. As they passed, Piave quoted the first two lines:*
>> *La donna è mobile*
>> *Qual' piuma al vento.*
>
> *Piave's former mistress took up the song, improvising words on the spot:*
>> *E Piave   è un asino*
>> *And Piave is an   ass*
>> *Che val'   per   cento.*
>> *Who is worth nothing (Literally: "who is worth a hundred" but, as you shall see in Chapter Ten, many idioms don't make literal sense.*
>
> *("Opera Anecdotes", by Ethan Mordden, p. 56.)*

Here is another famous passage, this time from 'Cavalleria Rusticana'. Notice how the parts of speech are used.

TURIDDU IN **CAVALLERIA RUSTICANA:**

Viva	il	vino	ch'è		sincero,
Long live	the	wine	which	is	honest,
VERB	ART.	NOUN	PRON.	VERB	ADJECTIVE

Che	ci	allieta	ogni	pensiero,
Which	(for us)	lightens	every	thought,
PRONOUN	PRON.	VERB	ADJECT.	NOUN

E	che	affoga	l'umor'	nero
And	which	drowns	humor	black
CONJ.	PRON.	VERB	NOUN	ADJECTIVE

Nell'ebbrezza	tenera.
In the drunkenness	tender.
PREP. ART./ NOUN	ADJECTIVE.

Here is a passage from **Don Carlo**. The translation has been given. See if you can identify the parts of speech. (See Chapter Twelve for the correct answers.)

Al	chiostro	di	San	Giusto
At the	cloister	of	Saint	Just
— —	————	—	————————

ove	finì	la	vita
where	finished	(his) life
———	————	———

l'avo	mio	Carlo	quinto,
the ancestor	mine	Charles	fifth
— ———	———	——— ———

stanco	di	gloria	e	onor';
tired	of	glory	and	honor;

_____   __   _____   __   _____

la	pace	cerco	invan'
the	peace	I seek	in vain

___   _____   _____   _____

che	tanto	ambisce	il	cor.
which	so much	aspires to	the	heart.

(Which the heart aspires to so much).

_____   _____   _____   ___ _____

As you master the various parts of speech in the following sections of this book, you will find that it becomes easier and easier to make your way unaided through a libretto. There is something very tidy about the process: every word in the language has to fall into one of nine categories. Once you know these categories (and the specialized language of opera) you can fathom the most difficult passages. There is great satisfaction to be derived in understanding the original and not having to trust blindly to translations, which are often inaccurate and seldom, if ever, perfect.

Before looking at nouns and articles note that any translations given in this book will be literal i. e. word for word, and as close as possible to the original. This will produce **some very unnatural English** at times but it will have the advantage of showing you exactly what each word means. (It would be ideal for you to learn to perceive the original Italian directly without translating, and this will come...) Let's look at the first two parts of speech: nouns and articles.

I, II NOUNS AND ARTICLES

All nouns in Italian are either masculine or feminine. The masculine nouns usually end in "o"; the feminine nouns usually end in "a".

MASCULINE	FEMININE
il figlio (the son)	la figlia (the daughter)
il lido (the bank e. g., of a river, stream)	la larva (the ghost)
il braccio (the arm)	la forza (the power; 'police')
il chiostro (the cloister)	la sventura (the misfortune)

Masculine nouns beginning with "s" followed by a consonant or "z" have a different article: "lo".

lo sghiamazzo (the squacking)
lo sgelo (the thaw)
lo svago (the pleasant time, diversion)
lo spirto (the spirit)

With some exceptions (e. g., il poeta) masculine nouns form the plural by changing the final "o" to an "i":

il pozzo (the well)	becomes	i pozzi
il birro (the 'cop')	becomes	i birri
il lume (the light)	becomes	i lumi
il pensiero (the thought)	becomes	i pensieri

As for the articles which usually accompany these nouns, if the article is "il" in the singular, it becomes "i" in the plural (as above). If the article is "lo" in the singular, it becomes "gli" in the plural:

lo zio (the uncle)	becomes	gli zii
lo stupido	becomes	gli stupidi
lo spunto (the first glimmer)	becomes	gli spunti
lo speco (the cave)	becomes	gli spechi

24

Things are simpler for the feminine: the singular words usually end in "a"; the plurals of these same words end in "e"—

la	chiesa (the church)	becomes	le chiese
la	sposa (the bride)	becomes	le spose
la	sventura (misfortune)	becomes	le sventure
la	notte (the night)	becomes	le notti
la	fiamma (the flame)	becomes	le fiamme

One peculiarity worth remembering about nouns is that those beginning with an 's' followed by another consonant usually suggest something evil, sinister and/or ridiculous:

lo sbirro (a pejorative word for policeman)
lo sdegno (scorn)
lo sgherro (a hired thug)
la smania (madness, strange obsession): "Degli amanti le smanie derido" (Of lovers I scorn the strange ravings). The Duke in **Rigoletto** ('Questa o Quella').
lo strepito (noise, confusion)
la sventura (misfortune)

See how many of Alfredo's nouns you can identify (with genders) in the drinking song from **La Traviata**:

| 1 | Sì, | attenti | al | cantor'... |
| | Yes, | attentive | to the | singer... |

| 2 | Libiamo, | libiamo | ne' | lieti | calici |
| | Let's drink, | let's drink | in (the) | happy | goblets |

| 3 | Che | la | bellezza | infiora; |
| | Which | | beauty | embellishes; |

| 4 | E | la | fuggevol' | ora |
| | And | the | fleeting | hour |

5   S'inn<u>e</u>brii   a   volutt<u>à</u>!
    Let it become intoxicated to the point of voluptuousness!

6   Libi<u>a</u>m'   ne'   dolci   fr<u>e</u>miti
    Let's drink in the   sweet   tremblings

7   Che   s<u>u</u>scita   l'amore,
    Which   gives birth to   love,
    (Which love gives birth to).

8   Poichè   quell'<u>o</u>cchio   al   core
    Since   that   eye   to the   heart

9   Onnipotente   va...
    All-powerful   goes...

    NOUNS: **GENDERS:**

1. _____   _____
2. _____   _____
3. _____   _____
4. _____   _____
5. _____   _____
6. _____   _____
7. _____   _____
8. _____   _____
9. _____   _____

Check your answers in Chapter Twelve.

III PREPOSITIONS

The third part of speech, the preposition, shows a relationship between a noun/pronoun and a noun/pronoun. This relationship can involve such things as **possession** ("di": of); a **spatial connection** ("su": on; "tra": between), or **time** ("prima di": before).

In Italian there are basically two types of prepositions: (a) those which combine with articles (e. g., "di" and "il" combine to form "del"; "in" and "la" combine to form "nella") and (b) those which do not combine (e. g., "contro di": against; "senza" or "senza di": without).

Once you recognize the first type (**combining prepositions**) you will have taken a big step towards mastering operatic Italian because such prepositions are extremely common.

The prepositions which always combine with articles are:

IN (in); **SU** (on); **DI** (of); **DA** (from); **A** (at; to). In addition **CON** (with) and **PER** (through) sometimes combine.

The following table shows how typical nouns combine with the "combining prepositions":

SINGULAR

	il colle	lo scudo	l' ingrato	la vergine	l' anima
a	al colle	allo scudo	all' ingrato	alla vergine	all' anima
da	dal colle	dallo scudo	dall' ingrato	dalla vergine	dall' anima
di	del colle	dello scudo	dell' ingrato	della vergine	dell' anima
in	nel colle	nello scudo	nell' ingrato	nella vergine	nell' anima
su	sul colle	sullo scudo	sull' ingrato	sulla vergine	sull' anima

PLURAL

	i colli	gli scudi	gli ingrati	le vergini	le anime
a	ai colli	agli scudi	agli ingrati	alle vergini	alle anime
da	dai colli	dagli scudi	dagli ingrati	dalle vergini	dalle anime
di	dei colli	degli scudi	degli ingrati	delle vergini	delle anime
in	nei colli	negli scudi	negli ingrati	nelle vergini	nelle anime
su	sui colli	sugli scudi	sugli ingrati	sulle vergini	sulle anime
	(hills)	(shields;'coins')	(ingrates)	(virgins)	(souls)

It is hard to find an operatic passage which is not peppered with combining prepositions:

1. **Sulla**   tomba,   eterna   guerra!
   On the   tomb,   eternal   war!   (Enrico in
   Lucia di Lammermoor)

2. **Al**   cane!   **Al**   traditore!
   To the   dog!   To   the   traitor!
   (Get the dog!)   (Get the traitor!)   (Sc<u>a</u>rpia in **Tosca**)

3. **Al**   buio   non   si   trova.
   In the dark   'it can't be found'. (Rodolfo in **La Bohème**)

4. (...) guardo **sui**   tetti   e   in   cielo
   I look (out) on the roofs and in (the) sky (Mimi, **La Bohème**)

5. **Nell'**or<u>e</u>cchie   **della**   gente
   In the ears   of the   people   (Bas<u>i</u>lio in **Il Barbiere**)

6. **Dalla**   tua   pace la mia   depende
   From (i.e. on) your peace mine depends (Ott<u>a</u>vio, **Giovanni**)

7. Par'   **dalla**   tomba   uscita!
   She seems   from   the tomb   emerged (lit. come out)
   (**Lucia di Lammermoor**)

TEST YOURSELF

Translate the combining prepositions in the following passages.

1. Viva   il vino   spumeggiante
   Long live   the wine   sparkling (lit.: 'frothing")
   Nel   bicchi<u>e</u>re   scintillante!
   _____   glass   sparkling!

   Come   il   riso   **dell'**amante
   Like   the   laugh   _____ lover
   Mite   infonde   il gi<u>u</u>bilo. (Turiddu in **Cavaller<u>i</u>a**)
   Mildly   it infuses   jubilation.

28

2. Di   quella pira l'orrendo fuoco!
   ___ that   pyre the horrid fire!   (Manrico in **Il Trovatore**)

3. Tutti   lo   seguono,
   All   him   follow,
   Grandi   e   ragazzi,
   Adults   and   boys,

   E   ognun'   applaude
   And   everyone   applauds
   Ai moti,   **ai** lazzi.
   ____ witticisms, ____ pranks. (The Chorus in **I Pagliacci**)

4. **Nei**   cieli   bigi   guardo   fumar'
   ___   skies   grey   I watch   smoke
   dai   mille   comignoli Parigi.
   _____ thousand chimneypots Paris. (Mimi in **La Bohème**)

5. In   due   passi
   In   two   steps
   Da quella (camera) puoi   gir'.
   ___   that   bedroom   you can go.   (**Figaro in Le Nozze**)

The second type of preposition does not combine with the definite article. Typical of this kind are the following:

fino a or sino a: up to, as far as
"(...) **sino** all'elsa questa lama/ vibra, immergi all'empio in cor'!"
Up to the hilt this blade/ stick it in the wicked man's heart!
(Azucena to Manrico in **Il Trovatore**)

fra or tra: between
"**Tra** voi saprò dividere / Il tempo mio giocondo."
Amongst you I will know how to allot my joyous time.
(Violetta to her guests in **La Traviata**)

intorno or d'intorno: around, surrounding
"(...) pari sono/A quant'altre **d'intorno** mi vedo."
...equal they are/To however many others 'around me' I see.
(The Duke in **Rigoletto,** 'Questa o Quella')

presso: near
"...**presso** la fonte..."
...near the fountain.
(Lucia in **Lucia di Lammermoor**)

prima (or prima di): before
"Cento trappole/**Prima di** cedere/Farò giocar'."
A hundred traps/Before giving in/I'll 'bring into play'.
(Rosina to herself in **Il Barbiere.**)

senza: without
"**Senza** strepito..."
Without noise...
Sparafucile, the hired assassin, describing to Rigoletto how he kills his victims. Nice neat work!

sopra (sovra): over, above, on
"La fatal' pietra **sovra** me si chiuse."
The fatal stone over me has 'closed itself'.
(Radamès in the tomb in **Aïda**)

sotto: under
"Sotto il pubblico flagello   (...) va   a   crepar'."
Under the public   'whip'   (...) goes (off) to 'croak'.
(Basilio in **Il Barbiere**)

Many great composers were perfectionists who hectored and bullied their librettists. RAI's (Radio-televisione Italiana's) Life of Verdi' shows an amusing scene in which Piave, alone, (you can hear his wife screaming shrilly at him and at their children in the background) reacts to a letter from Verdi in which the composer dictates to his librettist exactly how he wants the **Macbeth** *libretto to be. Looking at Verdi's actual correspondence we catch many a glimpse of his refusal to compromise. In the following extract Verdi wryly berates Ghislanzoni for failing to understand the kind of language which would be appropriate -- psychologically and dramatically -- for the final scene in which Radamès enters his tomb only to discover Aïda there:*

"Radamès would not be in the mood to utter phrases like 'I am separated from the living for ever.' 'No more splendors will my sight behold.' (...) I should like to avoid the usual death agonies and not have words like 'I'm failing. I'm going before you. Wait for me. She is dead. I'm still alive.' etc. I should like something sweet, otherwordly, a very short duet, a farewell to life."

Verdi goes on to give the actual words that he wants for Radamès: "Here is my tomb. (...) I will never see Aïda again." etc. These are the very words which will find their place in the final **Aïda** *libretto. They are the right words because they are natural and come straight from the heart. Ghislanzoni's words are forced and unnatural. How fortunate it is that Verdi was such a stickler and insisted on directing the details of the libretto! (Letter of Dec. 1870, quoted by Osborne -- p.105.)*

As for Puccini, Illica, one of his librettists, had this to say about him: "To work for Puccini means to go through a living hell. Not even Job could withstand his whims and his sudden volte-faces. (...) As for the libretto, it has been rewritten in its entirety three times, and some passages have been rewritten as many as four or five times."
(Dante del Fiorentino: "Immortal Bohemian").

Top left: Metastasio (1698-1782), the major influence on Italian opera librettos. See p. 1.

Top right: Piave, Verdi's great librettist. See pp. 45, 48.

Bottom: two scenes from RAI's first-rate **Life of Verdi**: the composer with Giuseppina Strepponi, his second wife; the composer as a young man standing in front of La Scala.

Top: Verdi, Strepponi and some of the **Nabucco** cast. (RAI).
Bottom: Cavaradossi singing **E Lucevan le Stelle**. (see p. 95)

Top: Iago (Sherrill Milnes) singing his "Credo". (See p. 131).
Bottom: Rigoletto (Louis Quilico) with Gilda (Maria Pellegrini). "Ite di qua!..."
31 c

Top: 'Il Cavallo Scalpita...' from **Cavalleria Rusticana**. See p. 136.
Bottom: Verdi's funeral, Milan. See page 104.

31 d

IV ADJECTIVES

The fourth part of speech, the adjective, is easy to identify but often very complex in meaning. This is particularly true of operatic adjectives. Because of this complexity I have devoted several pages to those which are typically problematic. With regard to form, adjectives change to suit the noun/pronoun which they describe. "Casto" (chaste) is typical. Here are its forms:

casto amore	(masc. singular)	**casti amori**	(masc. plural)
casta diva	(fem. singular)	**caste dive**	(fem. plural)

The masculine ends in "o"; the feminine ends in "a". This is the most common kind of adjective, but there are also those which end in "e" in both the masculine and the feminine singular. "Gentile" ('nice', pleasant, well-born) is typical:

guerriero gentile	(masc. sing.)	guerrieri gentili	(masc. plur.)
donna gentile	(femin. sing.)	donne gentili	(fem. plural)

A few other adjectives end in "e": fedele (faithful); felice (happy); migliore (better); sorridente (smiling).

Opera is a realm of complex feelings and often conflicting emotions, which are rather abstract, mysterious things. No part of speech reflects this better than the adjective. Mr. Rodney Milnes sums it up well in his comment on **Il Trovatore:**

"(...) a masterpiece as a text written to be sung—short lines, wonderfully linked. But you couldn't perform it as a play; it's quite abstract..." (from **Opera Today,** p. 286)

It is mainly its adjectives (orrido, funesto, orrendo, insano, misero, rio, indegno, etc.) which give **Il Trovatore** this peculiar abstract quality. Doubtless it was largely to adjectives that Verdi was referring when he urged his librettist, Ghislanzoni, to find "theatrical words":

32

"I don't know if I can explain what I mean by 'theatrical word' but I think I mean the word that most clearly and neatly brings the stage situation to life. (...) if the action calls for it, I would immediately abandon rhythm, rhyme and stanza. I would use blank verse in order to be able to say clearly and distinctly what the action requires."
(Charles Osborne, "Letters to Verdi" pp.159-160)

The following adjectives are typically operatic i. e. often violent and vague, but always dramatic and rich both in connotation and in their power to create atmosphere (this vagueness makes them one of the most difficult aspects of the libretto to master.) Although not exhaustive, the following list contains many of the typically complex operatic adjectives. A knowledge of them will prove very useful in reading librettos and it is well worth the effort to devote considerable time to them.

COMMON OPERATIC ADJECTIVES

altero (aloof, arrogant):
"Misterioso, **altero** / Croce e delizia..."
Mysterious, aloof / Cross i.e. crucifix and delight...
(Alfredo in **La Traviata**)

aspro (bitter, rough, harsh):
"Mal' reggendo all'**aspro** assalto..."
Badly holding up to the bitter attack...
(Manrico to Azucena in **Il Trovatore**)

baldo (bold, made bold):
"**baldi** dalla facil' vittoria..."
made bold by the easy victory
(Messenger to the 'King' in **Aïda**)

bramato (desired, lusted after):
"La cosa **bramata** proseguo..."
The thing lusted after I pursue...
(Scarpia in **Tosca**)

candido (white; pure):
"La bella mano **candida**..."
What a beautiful white hand!
(The Duke to Maddalena in **Rigoletto**)

cupo (mysterious, 'spooky'):
"In notte **cupa** la mente è perduta...."
In the dark night the mind is lost...
(Aïda to herself)

ebbro (drunk; crazed with desire)
Maddelena: "**Ebbro**!" The Duke: "D'amor' ardente!"
Drunk! (...) With ardent love! (**Rigoletto**)

egro (sick; weak):
"Del prigioniero misero / Conforta l'**egra** mente!"
Of the wretched prisoner / Comfort the sick mind!
(Leonora to herself in **Il Trovatore**)

empio (impious, disrespectful):
"...dal mio labbro/uscì l'**empia** parola!"
...from my lip/emerged the impious word!
(Aïda to herself in 'Ritorna Vincitor')

enorme (extraordinary, very strange):
Marullo: "Caso **enorme**!" (What an extraordinary happening!) The other courtiers: "Perduto ha la gobba?" (Has he lost his hump?)
(Speaking of Rigoletto, of course.)

fiero (terrible, frightening):
"...i **fieri** eventi e i lunghi tuoi dolor'..."
the terrible events and your long sufferings...
(Desdemona to Otello)

fosco (dark, i.e. 'sinful'):
"...i **foschi** baci/ Di quel selvaggio..."
...the **sin**ful kisses of that savage.
(Iago to Roderigo in **Otello**)

34

fugace (fleeting, short-lived):
"Godiam', **fugace** e rapido..."
Let's take our pleasure, fleeting and ephemeral...
(Violetta in **La Traviata**)

fulgido (resplendent, sparkling):
"Poi mi guidavi ai **fulgidi** deserti.."
"Then you guided me to the shimmering deserts..."
(Desdemona to Otello)

funesto (deadly, harmful, unlucky):
"Cruda, **funesta** smania..."
cruel, deadly 'obsession'...
(Enrico to Normanno in **Lucia**)

gentile (noble, courtly, gracious, kind):
"La calunnia è un venticello,/Un'auretta assai **gentile**..."
Calumny is a little wind,/A very nice little breeze...
(Basilio to Bartolo in **Il Barbiere**)

ignoto (unknown):
"Vissi **d'ignoto** amor'..."
I lived i. e. survived on an unknown love...
(Alfredo to Violetta in **La Traviata**)

indarno (in vain):
"E furo **indarno** / Tante ricerche e tante!"
And they were in vain / So many, many searches!
(The Count in **Il Trovatore**)

leggiadro (beautiful, elegant, gracious, confident,
sophisticated, poised, etc.):
"Sempre un amabile, / **leggiadro** viso..."
Always an amiable, beautiful face.
(The Duke in **Rigoletto**: 'La Donna è Mobile')
Notice how many words I have had to use in order to
even approximate the meaning of "leggiadro".

lieto (happy, cheerful):
"Libiamo ne' **lieti** calici / che la bellezza infiora!"
Let's drink in the happy goblets / which beauty
(Alfredo in **La Traviata**)   /embellishes!

mesto (discontented, grief-ridden):
"Come sei **mesta**!"
How sad you are!
(Emilia to Desdemona in **Otello**)

misero (wretched, unhappy, unfortunate):
"Giovanna, Giovanna! Ahi! **Misera**!"
Giovanna, Giovanna! Alas! Wretch!
(Gilda in **Rigoletto**)

orrendo (horrid):
"Di quella pira l'**orrendo** fuoco..."
Of that pyre the horrid fire.
(Manrico to Leonora in **Il Trovatore**)

regio (royal):
"O Re, se non foss'io / con te nel **regio** ostel'..."
Oh, King, if I weren't with you in the royal 'palace'...
(The Grand Inquisitor to Philip in **Don Carlo**)

reo / rio (evil, ill-starred, guilty):
"Trema! O **rea** schiava!"
Tremble! oh evil slave!
(Amneris to Aïda).

spietato (pitiless).
As mentioned in connection with 's-impure' nouns,
's-impure' adjectives usually have a negative
connotation.

EXAMPLES:

spavaldo (arrogant)

stolto (stupid)

stordito (stunned, stupified):
"Lasciatemi, **stordito**!" (Leave me alone, you 'nut case'!)
(Maddalena to the Duke, **Rigoletto**)

stralunato (crazy, weird, wild-looking):
"Quel' Masetto mi par' **stralunato**."
That Masetto seems to me 'out of his gordita'.
(Zerlina in **Don Giovanni**)

straziato (torn to pieces, tormented)

strepitoso (noisy)

sventurato (unlucky):
"Ah! **sventurata**! Che dissi?"
Ah, wretch! what did I say?   (Aïda to herself).

tetro (dark, sad, horrible):
"Sinistra splende /Sui volti orribili/ la **tetra** fiamma..."
Sinister, shines on the horrible faces the 'dark, grim' flame...).
(Azucena, **Trovatore**: 'Stride la Vampa'). Note atmosphere!

torbido (troubled, turbulent, etc.):
"Mille **torbidi** pensieri..."
(Donna Anna and Ottavio in **Don Giovanni**)

tremendo (frightening, terrible):
"Nella città dei Cesari/ **tremendo** echeggerà."
In the city of the Caesars/Will echo in a frightening way.
(The Druids in **Norma**)

triste (sad, pathetic):
"Brevi e **tristi** giorni visse..."
Short and sad days he lived...
(Ferrando to soldiers in **Il Trovatore**)

truce (menacing, sinister, ghastly, cruel):
"al pensier' s'affaccia   Il **truce** caso."
to the mind ('thought') presents itself / The ghastly event.
(Azucena in **Il Trovatore**)

vezzoso (beautiful, gracious, comely, charming):
"La piccina è ognor' **vezzosa**."
The petite woman is always charming.
(Leporello in **Don Giovanni**)

In addition, the following adjectives are as common in opera as their equivalents are in English:

questo (this)	quello (that)	quale (which)

mio	(my)	nostro	(our)	
tuo	(your)	vostro	(your)	(POSSESSIVE ADJECTIVES)
suo	(her/his/its)	loro	(their)	

"Vostro" is used for both the familiar plural and the respectful singular form of "you" (i.e. where the modern Italian would use "Lei")." Il **vostro** vino io non l'accetto.."(I don't accept your wine..) (Alfio to Turiddu in **Cavalleria Rusticana**)

Hundreds more adjectives are formed from the **past participles** of verbs. "Cingere" (the infinitive of the verb meaning "to gird, to wreathe") has the irregular past participle "cinto" (girded, wreathed)."Di lauri cinto" as Radamès says of Aïda. "Spargere" (the infinitive of the verb meaning "to intersperse with, to bedeck") has the irregular past participle "sparso", which can be used as an adjective. Pollione describes Adalgisa's hair as "sparsa di fior(i)..." i.e. bedecked with flowers (**Norma**)

Notice the power of the past participles used in **Il Barbiere**:

avvilito (from **avvilire**, to revile).
calpestato (from **calpestare**, to stomp on).
calunniato (from **calunniare**, to slander):

"E il meschino **calunniato**,
And the slandered 'pathetic little man',

Avvilito, calpestato,
Reviled, stomped on,

Sotto il pubblico flagello,
Under the public scourge, (whip)

Per gran' sorte va a crepar'."
Through (this) great luck i. e. 'if he's lucky!'
goes off (somewhere) to 'croak'. (Don Basilio)
(See photo, p. 49).

This translation is about as close as I can get to Cesare Sterbini's libretto. Compare the following translation (taken from a very good modern recording of the opera): "So the victim of your slander/Can do nothing but surrender/ To the public indignation/At his impropriety." This kind of translation amounts to a clever Gilbert-and-Sullivanesque effort to create in English a paraphrase which will be idiomatic and maybe even rhythmically suited to being sung in English. There is nothing wrong with that, as long as one remembers how far such versions stray from the original Italian and its **much wilder flair;** the Rossini/Sterbini version suggests (with violent words like "calpestato", "flagello", and "crepar'") that society at large is unkind, indeed even cruel, to those unfortunate enough to find themselves the victims of unfounded gossip. As I wrote earlier, (pp. 4, 5) the original Italian is not only better than any translation; it also contains innuendos and carries implications which are lost or ignored in any translation.

A few other past participles as adjectives:

ingannato (tricked, cheated):
"...ma se da lui **ingannata** rimasi?..."
(...but if by him i. e. Don Giovanni I was tricked?...)
(Zerlina to Masetto in **Don Giovanni**)

sconsigliato (ill-advised, rash, foolish):
"Sconsigliata!"
(Don Giovanni to Donna Anna)

temprato (tempered):
"il sacro brando dal Dio **temprato**..."
(the sacred sword tempered by the God).
(Ramfis to Radamès in Aïda)

traviato: he who has strayed from the 'path'.
(**La Traviata**...)

Of all the parts of speech, the adjective probably does the most to create atmosphere, set a tone, develop character, and introduce a theme. Perhaps this is so because of the richness and vagueness of many operatic adjectives ("cupo": "dark, mysterious, 'spooky', is typical). Certain adjectives occur with great frequency in a given opera and acquire the force of unifying symbols and/or emotional leit-motivs. "Lieto" (happy), "fuggevole" (fleeting), and "egro" (sick) are quintessential **Traviata**; the very mention of "possente" (powerful), "costante" (faithful, constant), and "dannato" (damned) bring to mind **Rigoletto**. "Degno/indegno" (worthy/unworthy), "sciagurato" (wretched) and "sconsigliato" (ill-advised) conjure up **Don Giovanni**.

V ADVERBS

Although not as plentiful nor as colorful as adjectives, adverbs nonetheless have a vital role to play and familiarity with the more common ones will do a lot to unlock the libretto for you. Their function is usually to answer questions like "How?", "When?", "How often?", "Where?", "How much?", "How many?", "To what degree?" The following are typical:

(1) **How?** e.g.   "**Cheti**, cheti, rubiamgli   l'amante!"
    Quietly, quietly, let's steal from him the lover
    (The courtiers in **Rigoletto**)

(2) **When?**, e.g.   "E tu non   sorgi   **ancora**,
    And you don't rise   yet,
    E   puoi   dormir' così."
    And you can   sleep   thus."
    (The Count in **Il Barbiere**.)
    Note that 'ancora' is an adverb of time;
    'così', an adverb of manner.

(3) **How often?**   "Ella **giammai**   m'amò!"
    She   never   loved me!
    (Philip to himself in **Don Carlo**)

(4) **Where?** e.g.,
"...e **qui** la luna
and here the moon
l'abbiamo vicina."
we have it near.
(Rodolfo to Mimi in **La Bohème**)

(5) **How much?**
"E **quanto** spendere per un signor' dovrei?"
And how much to spend for a lord would I
have (to)?
How much would I have to spend for a lord?
(Rigoletto to Sparafucile.)

(6) **Which?** e.g.,
"**Ogni** villa, ogni borgo, ogni paese
Every villa, every village, every country
È (è) testimon' di sue donnesche imprese."
Is witness of his 'woman-directed' exploits.
(Leporello to Donna Elvira in **Don Giovanni**)

There are other functions of adverbs too, but these six are the main ones and if you can recognize these, you probably can recognize most others.

As to form, the adverb is theoretically formed by adding "mente" ("ly" in English) to the feminine singular adjective:

destra (dextrous, adroit) expands to **destramente** (dextrously, /adroitly).

However, in reality, not many adverbs used in opera end in "mente". Most look nothing like their adjectival cousins and must be learned on their own. The following are some of the adverbs which surface regularly in opera librettos. They are not that easy but the good news is that, unlike nouns and adjectives, **adverbs never change form to agree with anything**. For convenience I have divided adverbs into three main categories:

(1) adverbs of time;
(2) adverbs of place; and
(3) adverbs of degree or manner.

(1) ADVERBS OF TIME

alfin' (finally):
"**Alfin'** sei mio." (Finally you are mine.)
Lucia.

ancora (still, again):
"Un'altra notte **ancora**/Senza vederlo!"
Yet another night/Without seeing him!
(Leonora in **Il Trovatore**)

dianzi :
(just a minute ago)
"... un messaggero/**Dianzi** giungea."
A messenger / Just now arrived.
(The 'King' in **Aïda**.)

già (already):
"**Già** mi mandi via"
You already send me away.
(Mimi to Rodolfo in **La Bohème**)

giammai (never):
"Non l'avrei **giammai** creduto!"
I never would have believed it!
(Don Giovanni to the Statue)

intanto (meanwhile):
"**Intanto** il marito fremendo se va..."
Meanwhile the husband trembling
(i.e. with rage and frustration) /goes away.
(Rigoletto in **Rigoletto**)

mai (never):
"Pur' **mai** non sentesi felice appieno."
Yet never does he feel completely happy.
(The Duke to himself in **Rigoletto**)

ognora (still):
"La piccina è **ognor'** vezzosa."
The petite woman is always charming.
(Leporello in **Don Giovanni**)

omai, ormai (by now):
"L'ombra **omai** del genitore/Pena avrà."
By now the shadow of the parent/Will have
sorrow. (Ottavio in **Don Giovanni**)

ora (now):
"Uscire?! Adesso?! /**Ora** che accendene un
fuoco istesso?!" (Leave?! Now?! /Now that
consumes us a veritable fire?)
('Gualtier Maldè' to Gilda in **Rigoletto**)

poi (then):
"**poi** la nave è bianca" (then the ship is
white). (Butterfly in **Madama Butterfly**:
'Un Bel Dì')

presto (quickly):
"**Presto**, qua il biglietto!" (Quickly, 'here'
the note!) (Figaro to Rosina in **Il Barbiere**)

42

sempre (always):	"**Sempre** libera!" Always free! (Violetta in **La Traviata**)
tosto (soon; quickly):	"Due cose, e **tosto**!" Two things, and quick! (The Duke to Sparafucile in **Rigoletto**)
tra (fra) **poco**: (before long)	"E pioverà **tra** poco." And it will rain before long. (Sparafucile to the Duke in **Rigoletto**)

(2) ADVERBS OF PLACE

dove, ove (where):	"...ecco la torre / **Ove** di Stato gemono i prigionieri." Behold the tower / Where of State groan i. e. languish, the prisoners. (Ruiz to Leonora, **Il Trovatore**)
fuori (outside):	"Io v'aspetto qui **fuori**." I await you here outside. (Alfio to Turiddu) in **Cavalleria Rusticana**)
là (there):	"È (è) **là**, non è vero?" She's there, isn't she? (Rigoletto to the Courtiers)
lassù (up there):	"**lassù** in cielo vicina alla madre..." Up there in Heaven, near Mother. (Gilda to Rigoletto)
lungi (far away):	"...**lungi** da me! Queste mie mani grondano sangue!" ...begone! / These hands of mine are dripping blood! (Alvaro to Leonora in **La Forza del Destino**)
qua; **qui** (here):	"Tu **qui** in questa tomba?" You here in this tomb? (Radamès to Aïda)

(3) ADVERBS OF DEGREE OR MANNER

alquanto
(a little while):

"**Alquanto** attendete."
Wait a moment.
(Sparafucile to Maddalena in **Rigoletto**)

appieno (fully, in full):

"Pur' mai non sentesi
Felice **appieno**..."
And yet never does he feel
Completely happy...
(The Duke in **Rigoletto**:
'La Donna è Mobile')

assai (very):

"Un'auretta **assai** gentile."
A little wind, very nice.
(Basilio to Bartolo in **Il Barbiere**)

come (how):

"**Come**? E donde?"
How? And where?
(The Duke to the Courtiers in **Rigoletto**)

così (thus):

"**Così** fan' tutte"
Thus do (behave) all of them,
i. e. all ladies.

male (badly):

"Lo dici **male**!"
You say it badly!
(Tosca to Cavaradossi in **Tosca**)

più (more):

"**Più** caldi baci avrà!"
Hotter kisses will he/she have.
(Alfredo In **La Traviata**)

quanto (how much):

"E **quanto** spendere
Per un signor' dovrei?"
(a) And how much (c) to spend
(d) For a gentleman? (b) would I have
(Rigoletto to Sparafucile in **Rigoletto**)

soltanto (only):

"Vi conosco da un anno **soltanto**."
I have known you for only a year.
(The Barone to Violetta in **La Traviata**.)

tanto (so much; so):

"lui ch'amo pur' **tanto**"
he whom I love so much.
(Aïda in 'Ritorna Vincitor!')

*"Years later he (Verdi) referred to **Rigoletto** as 'my best opera', and in a letter to a Neapolitan friend he praised the libretto, too.'One of the most beautiful librettos that exist,' he wrote, then added a slight jab at his friend Piave: 'except for the verses.'"*

*(Quoted by William Weaver in "Verdi Librettos".) This helps explain why I have quoted so much from **Rigoletto**!*

PURE

Before leaving adverbs, special mention should be made of "pure". "Pure" is its own phantom of the opera, surfacing in many disguises and taking on many meanings: and; go ahead; even; and yet; just now; surely. The extracts below will show it at work.

(1) AND
   "...a noi **pure** una voce / Di perdono dal cielo verrà."
   to us too a voice /   of pardon from Heaven will come.
   (Gilda to Rigoletto)
(2) GO AHEAD
   "Fremi **pure**, e angoscia eterna **pur'** m'imprechi il tuo furor'!"
   Go ahead and tremble, and let your fury curse me with eternal anguish.
   (Pollione to Norma in **Norma**)
(3) EVEN
   "O, se **pur** disarmata,/ Questa man' per voi fora cruenta."
   Or, if even disarmed,/ This hand   for you will be cruel.
   (Rigoletto to the Courtiers)
(4) STILL, AND YET
   "**Pur'** quel voto   non è   infranto
   And yet that vow is not   broken
   (Edgardo to Lucia in **Lucia di Lammermoor**)

(5) JUST NOW (A MOMENT AGO)
"Io che **pur'** piansi, or' rido."
I who just now cried, now I laugh.
(Rigoletto to the Courtiers).

(6) SURELY, CERTAINLY
"Siamo **pure** i deboli di testa!"
We are surely the weak 'in the' head!
(Don Giovanni)
"Il Duca qui **pur'** si diverte!"
The Duke here certainly is amusing himself!
(Borsa and the Courtiers in **Rigoletto**)

(7) 'PURE' AS A CONVENIENT GAP-FILLER.
As incredible as it might sound, "pure" sometimes means absolutely nothing. It sounds good, however, and is a useful pleonasm or gap-filler (see pp. 8, 129) for the librettist who needs to expand the words to fit the musical phrase:

"Compiuto **pur'** quanto a fare mi resta
Having completed however much there remains for me to do
Lasciare potremo quest'aura funesta."
We will be able to leave this fatal atmosphere."
(Rigoletto to Gilda)

We have now looked at five parts of speech: articles, nouns, prepositions, adjectives, and adverbs. See if you can identify all five in the following three extracts (See Chapter Twelve for the answers.)

First, Basilio's magnificent bass aria on how to destroy your rival:

(1) No? Uditemi e tacete.
No? Listen to me and be silent.
VERB/PRON. CONJUNCTION VERB

La calunnia è un venticello,
Slander is a little wind,
_____ VERB _____ _____

Un'	auretta	assai	gentile
A little	breeze	very	nice
— _____		_____	_____

Che	insensibile,	sottile,
Which	imperceptible,	subtle,
CONJUNCTION	_____	_____

Leggermente,	dolcemente
Lightly,	sweetly
_____	_____

Incomincia,	incomincia	a	susurrar'.
Begins,	begins	to	whisper.
VERB	VERB	___	VERB

(Basilio, **Il Barbiere**).

Tosca's plea for mercy to the villainous Scarpia:

(2)
Vissi	d'arte,	vissi	d'amore,
I lived	on art,	I lived	on love,
VERB	___ ____	VERB	___ _____

Non	feci	mai	male	ad	anima	viva!
I never	did		evil	to	(a) living	soul!
VERB	____		____	___	_____	_____

Con	man'	furtiva,	quante	pene	conobbi,	alleviai.
With	furtive hand,'as many'			griefs	I knew of,	I 'lightened'.
—	____	_____	_____	_____	VERB,	VERB.

Sempre	con	fè'	sincera	la	mia	preghiera
Always	with	faith	sincere		my	prayer
_____	___	_____	_____	___	___	_____

ai	santi	tabernacoli	salì.
at the	holy	altars	rose.
— ___	____	_____	VERB

(Tosca in **Tosca**).

47

Radamès' noble longings for glory and love in 'Celeste Aïda':

(3) Celeste   Aïda,   forma   divina,
     Heavenly   Aida,   divine   form,
     _____   _____   _____   _____

     Mistico   serto   di   luce   e   fior',
     Mystical garland of   light   and   flower(s),
     _____   _____   __   ___   CONJUNCTION_____

     Del   mio   pensiero   tu   sei   regina.
     Of   my   thought   you   are   queen.
     ___   ____ _____   PRONOUN   VERB   _____.

     Tu   di   mia   vita   sei   lo   splendor'.
     You   of   my   life   are   the   splendor.
     PRON. __   ____ ____ VERB   ___   _____

     Il tuo bel   cielo vorrei   ridarti--
     Your beautiful sky I would like to give back to you--
     ___   _____   ____VERB   VERB & PRONOUN

     Le   dolci   brezze   del   patrio   suol'.
     The   sweet   breezes of the 'fatherland' soil.
     ___   _____   _____   _____   _____   _____

*Maybe we'll never know how the librettist's mind conceived those beautiful lines, but RAI's "Life of Verdi" contains a superb (apocryphal) passage which imaginatively surmises the paths which Piave's mind might well have followed as he refined the libretto to **La Traviata**; it is a question of the famous scene in which Alfredo's father urges Violetta to renounce his son while she in turn tries to impress upon Germont Senior how difficult such a renunciation would be for her.*

*Here's Piave thinking: "You ask that I forget him forever. And then what?! Love is not a pact! (...) You cannot know the cruel turn that my existence has been dealt...that my existence has been dealt...The morbid turn...the malaise...**malady**...the morbid turn... You cannot imagine the malady that has plagued my life... the fierce malady...No! The **dark** malady! The **dark** malady that plagues me! You can't imagine the affection, the vivid passion within my breast!..." RAI's portrayal of Piave is convincing: a self-deprecating, good-humoured perfectionist whose persistence and talent led him on in a relentless search for just the right word, just the right 'parola lirica' for Verdi.*

Don Basilio singing 'La Calunnia...' from **Il Barbiere**. See p. 38-9.

CHAPTER FOUR

The sixth part of speech, the pronoun, replaces the noun and functions in a similar way. One of the most chameleon-like parts of speech, the pronoun changes aspect according to its use in the sentence. This makes the pronoun rather difficult. For example, in the following sentences all the underlined pronouns refer to the speaker: I (io). The only reason these pronouns look different is because they have different functions in the sentence:

(1) "**Io** vo' mia figlia!" (I want my daughter.)
      Io is the subject pronoun, the 'doer' of the action.
      (Rigoletto to the Courtiers)
(2) "Chi **mi** frena in tal' momento?"
      Who stops me at such a moment?
      "Mi" is the direct object pronoun,
      the 'receiver' of the action. (Edgardo in the deliriously
      powerful sextet from **Lucia di Lammermoor**.)
(3) "Quel che a lei piace / Vita **mi** rende...
      Whatever pleases her / Gives back life to me...
      "Mi" is the indirect object pronoun, the person(s) who
      receives the direct object, which in this case is "vita".
      (Don Ottavio in **Don Giovanni**)
(4) "Per **me** pari sono..." (For me are the same...)
      "Me": object of the preposition "per". (The Duke)
(5) "È (è) desso, o pur' **m**'inganno?"[1]
      Is it he or am I fooling myself?
      "Mi" is the reflexive object.
      ingannarsi: to fool oneself.
      (The Count to himself in **Il Barbiere**).
(6) "Ella **mi** fu rapita!" (She was abducted from me!)
      "Mi" has the form of an indirect object but it functions
      as a '**dative of advantage**'.
      These very important beasts will be explained below.
      (The Duke to himself in **Rigoletto**).

---

[1] Note the 'd' on 'desso'. This is for sound (euphony).

As you can see from the above, there are six main ways in which **personal pronouns** can be used. The following tables outline the six forms; illustrative examples follow.

I SUBJECT PERSONAL PRONOUNS

SINGULAR	PLURAL
(1) io (I)	noi (we)
(2) tu (you)	voi (you--plur. or
(3) egli, ei, desso, esso (he)	/formal sing.)
essa, dessa (she)	essi, loro (they)
ella (she or you--formal).	esse (they/fem.)

The subject pronouns act as the subject of a sentence or a clause.

Examples:

(a) "Eri **tu** che macchiavi quell'anima!"
It was you who defiled that soul!
(**Un Ballo in Maschera**)
("Macchiavi" contains "chiavi", the "f-word"...)
When you know the language, this kind of (apt) con-
notation is inescapable. See the footnote on page 3.

(b) "Presto, presto, pria ch'**ei** venga!"
Quick, quick, before he comes! (**Don Giovanni**)

(c) "**Io** ne' volumi arcani leggo del cielo."
I in the volumes arcane read about heaven.
(Norma to Oroveso, the Druids, etc. in **Norma**.)

Actually these subject pronouns are often omitted because it is clear from the form of the verb used what the subject must be:

"Bramo, la cosa bramata proseguo, me ne sazio..."
I lust, the thing lusted after I follow, I fill myself
with it... (There is no need for Scarpia -- in **Tosca**
-- to identify himself by the pronoun "io" because it
is clear who is meant.)

On the other hand, the use of the **subject pronoun** with the verb can add emphasis. When Rigoletto, beside himself with grief, fear, and rage, asks for Gilda to be released to him, the pronoun "io" adds much strength to his plea ("**Io** vo' mia figlia!" I want my daughter!) Alfio's defiant "**io** non l'accetto!" to Turiddu (see p. 38) is the same kind of thing.

II DIRECT OBJECT PERSONAL PRONOUNS

	SINGULAR	PLURAL
1	mi (me)	ci, ne (us)
2	ti (you, thee)	vi (you)
3	lo, il (him, it)	li or gli (masc. plur.): them.
	la (her, it)	le (fem. pl.): them.

The **direct object** pronouns directly receive the action of the verb.

Examples:

(a) "Qui **ne** condusse ridevol' cosa..."
Here us led (a) laughable thing...
A laughable thing led us here ...
(Marullo to Rigoletto)
"Ne" is strictly operatic/old-fashioned and is
no longer used in spoken Italian. "Ci", on the other
hand, is still very much part of the spoken language.
(b) "Deh, **il** salvate!"
For pity's sake, save him!
(Carlo to Surgeon in **La Forza del Destino**).
(c) "Più l'adorata vergine/io non **la** trova accanto."
Non longer the adored virgin/do I find (her)
beside (me).
(Pollione to Flavio in **Norma**).

III INDIRECT OBJECT PERSONAL PRONOUNS

SINGULAR
1   mi (to me)
2   ti (to you, to thee)
     gli (to him)
     le (to her; to you)

PLURAL
ci, ce, ne (to us)
vi, ve (to you)
loro (to them)

Indirect object pronouns (or "datives", as grammarians call them) closely resemble direct object pronouns except that the indirect type refers to a person(s) to whom something is given, conveyed, said, etc.

Examples:

(a) "Signorina, **le** dirò con due parole..."
     Miss, I will tell you with two words...
     (Rodolfo to Mimi in **La Bohème**).
(b) "...Santa, allor' grato **vi** sono."
     Santa, then I am grateful to you.
     (Alfio to Santuzza in **Cavalleria Rusticana**.)
(c) "Dim**mi** tu dove l'hanno nascosta."
     You tell me where they have hidden her.
     (Rigoletto to Marullo.)

IV   THE DATIVE OF ADVANTAGE

A special and very important use of the indirect object pronoun is called the "dative of advantage" (or "disadvantage") or "dative of interest". Opera librettos have as many such datives as a porcupine has quills, and although these datives are tricky, once you learn to identify them your understanding of opera will take a huge leap. Datives of advantage suggest that the person involved is either **benefitting from an action or suffering from the consequences of one**. English still occasionally uses these datives (e. g. the song: "Cry me a River!") but they are not nearly as common as they once were (Shakespeare uses them all the time, as in King Lear's line about drawing an arrow properly: "Draw me a clothier's yard!" (Act III).

53

Examples:
(a) "Ella **mi** fu rapita!"
She 'to my detriment' was abducted!
(The Duke to himself, in **Rigoletto**).

(b) "Cheti, cheti, rubiam**gli** l'amante!"
Quiet, quiet, let's steal "to his detriment" the lover!
(The courtiers in **Rigoletto**).

(c) "La costoro avvenenza è qual' dono
Their comeliness is like (a) gift
Di che il fato **ne** infiora la vita."
'With' which fate 'to our benefit' embellishes life.
(The Duke in **Rigoletto** --'Questa o Quella').

(d) "Di quale nobil' fierezza / **Ti** balena il volto."
With what noble pride/ To your advantage your face
lights up. (Amneris to Radamès, in **Aïda**)

(e) "Un gelo **mi** serpeggia nel sen'."
'Icy coldness' (to my detriment) winds itself
in my breast.
(Lucia to herself, **Lucia di Lammermoor**)

(f) "Carlo **mi** colma il cor'/ d'una tristezza amara!"
Carlo 'for me' fills my heart/ with a sadness bitter!
(Philip to the Grand Inquisitor in **Don Carlo**)

V INDIRECT AND DIRECT
OBJECT PRONOUNS TOGETHER

When these two pronouns come together, the indirect will come first and the two will often combine to form one word:

(a) "**Mel** dice da quel verone
To me says from that balcony
Tremante un raggio
Trembling a ray
Della notturna lampa."
Of the nocturnal lamp (i. e. the moon)."
(The Conte di Luna in **Il Trovatore**). Note the typically twisted structure of these verses.

54

(b) "Io **ve l'**ho detto. E (è) il titolo dell'opera novella."
I said it to you. It's the title of the new opera."
(Figaro in **Il Barbiere**)

VI REFLEXIVE PRONOUNS

	SINGULAR	PLURAL
(1)	**mi** cangio	**ci** cangiamo
	I change myself	we change ourselves
(2)	**ti** cangi	**vi** cangiate
	you change yourself	you change yourself/ves
(3)	**si** cangia (s/he changes	**si** cangiano
	him/herself, etc.)	they change themselves

"In altro uom' **mi** cangio."
Into another man I change myself.
(Rigoletto to himself).

The **reflexive pronoun** (myself, yourself, himself, herself, etc.)
forms part of the reflexive verb and will be dealt with again in the
verb section (pages 71-72.) Although reflexives are rare in English
they are **very common in operatic Italian** (and in modern Italian).

Examples:
(a) "Vorrei   pregar'
    I would like to pray
    Ma la mia prece   in bestemmia **si muta**
    (from **mutarsi**).
    But   my prayer   in blasphemy transforms itself.
    (Aïda to herself).
(b) "(...) sforzati! / Bah, sei tu forse   un uom'?!"
    Force yourself!/ Bah, are you perhaps a man?!
    (Canio to himself in **Pagliacci**).

VI DISJUNCTIVE PRONOUNS

SINGULAR	PLURAL
(1) me (me)	noi (us)
(2) te (you)	voi (you)
(3) lui, esso (masc.)	loro (masc. or fem.)
lei, essa (fem.)	essi (masc.)
se (himself, herself, itself)	esse (fem.)

Disjunctives are used after a preposition (**con, per**, etc.). Unlike the pronouns in sections I to V above, they do not combine with the verb. They are easy to identify and require little explanation.

Examples:
(a) "Beva con **me**!"
Drink with me! (Iago to Cassio in **Otello**)
(b) "Tremo per **te**, fellon'!"
I tremble for you, you traitor!
(Norma to Pollione in **Norma**)

VII OTHER KINDS OF PRONOUNS

The main personal pronouns have been explained above. There are four other kinds of pronouns as well, but they are easy to grasp and their meaning should be clear from context.

A. POSSESSIVE PRONOUNS

SINGULAR	PLURAL
(1) il mio, la mia, etc.	il nostro, la nostra, etc.
(2) il tuo, la tua, etc.	il vostro, la vostra, etc.
(3) il suo, la sua, etc.	il loro, la loro

Possessive pronouns look much like the possessive adjectives mentioned on page 38. As usual, they agree in gender and number with the noun which they replace.

Examples:
(a) "Tosca finalmente (è) mia!"
    Tosca finally   (is) mine!
    (Scarpia to himself in **Tosca**)

(b) "Alfin' son' **tua!**"
    Finally   I am yours!
    (Lucia to Edgardo in **Lucia di Lammermoor**)

B. INTERROGATIVE PRONOUNS

Chi?   (Who?)   Che?   (What?)
Quale? (Which?)   Quanto? (How much?)

These are the pronouns for asking questions.

Examples:
(a) "**Chi** mi frena in tal' momento?"
    Who stops me   at such a moment?
    (Edgardo in the sextet, **Lucia di Lammermoor**)
(b) "Sì, la mia figlia!...   d'una tal' vittoria...
    Yes, my daughter!...   about such a victory...
    Che?...   adesso non ridete?"
    What?...   Now you aren't laughing?
    (Rigoletto to Courtiers)
(c) Sparafucile to Rigoletto: "E voi ne   avete."
                                 And you   have (a rival).
    Rigoletto to Sparafucile: "**Quale?**"
                                 Which? (i. e. Who?)
(d) Tosca to Scarpia: "**Quanto?**"
                                 How much?
    Scarpia to Tosca: "**Quanto?!**
                                 How much?!

C. RELATIVE PRONOUNS

che (who, whom, which, what)
cui (to whom, to which)

These pronouns link clauses:
    Examples:
    (a) "O mia povera Liu,
        Oh, my poor Liu,
        al tuo piccolo cuore **che** non cade
        to your little heart   which doesn't 'fall' (falter)
        chiede colui   **che** non sorride più!"
        asks he   who no longer smiles!
        (Il Principe to Liu in **Turandot**,
        'Nessun' Dorma!').

D. DEMONSTRATIVE PRONOUNS

questo (this one)	costui (that one over there -- masc.)
quello (that one)	costei (that one over there -- fem.)
colui (he who); colei (f.)	costoro (those people over there)

These pronouns usually point out a contrast: "questo" (this one), as opposed to "quello" (that one). Like all pronouns, these agree in gender and number with the noun which they replace.

    Examples:
    (a) "Questa o quella, a   me pari   sono!"
        This one or that one, to me   they are the same!
        (The Duke to Borsa in **Rigoletto**)
    (b) "Ah, suora non m'è   **colei!**"
        Ah, a sister she is not to me, that one! (i. e. Lucia)
        (Enrico in **Lucia di Lammermoor**)
        Note the hostility and detachment in "colei".

58

(c) "...che venne a fare **colui** questa mattina?"
...what did that one (Figaro) come to do this morning?
(Bartolo to Rosina) Note that "colui" usually has a
disparaging ring and reveals Bartolo's (well-founded!)
hostility.

E. A FEW PRONOUN IDIOMS

(a) "Per Bacco!" By Bacchus! (Figaro)
"Non **ci** credete?" Don't you believe it? (Rosina)
There is no explanation as to why the "**ci**" is needed;
it just is. We just have to shrug our shoulders and
say "It's an idiom..."
(More on this topic in Chapter Ten).

(b) "Che **ne** dite, mio signor'?
What do you say about it, my Lord?
Non vi par' che l'ho trovato?"
Doesn't it seem to you that I've found it?
(Figaro to the Count in **Il Barbiere**)

Note that "**ne**" can mean 'of it', 'about it', 'of them', 'about him',
and in its use closely resembles the French "**en**". Still, there's no
explaining **why** it has to be there; it just does!
As you have seen, there are many different pronouns. See how
many you can identify in the following extracts (The key is in
Chapter Twelve.):

1. "**Mi** chiamano Mimi."
They call me Mimi. Mi:_____
(Mimi to Rodolfo in **La Bohème**).

2. "Scusate**mi** se da sol' **mi** presento!"
Excuse me if alone I introduce myself! mi:_____mi:_____
(The Prologue in **I Pagliacci**)

3. "Isi   placata   **ti**   schiuda   il   ci̲e̲l'!"
   Let Isis, placated, open heaven for you! ti: _____
   (Amneris to Radam̲è̲s in **Aïda**)

4. "Gravi   novelle **ei** reca... **Vi** pia̲ccia udirlo!
   Serious news   he brings... May it please you to hear him!
   ei: _____   vi:_____   lo:_____
   (The "King" to the Egyptians in **Aïda**).

5. "D'amo̲r' **ti**   struggi   per Radam̲è̲s!"
   With love   you destroy yourself   for Radam̲è̲s!
   ti: _____
   (Amonasro to **Aïda**).

6. "È̲ (è) sempre mi̲sero   **chi**   a   **lei**   s'affida."
   He is   always   wretched whoever to her 'entrusts himself'.
   chi: _____   lei: _____   s': _____
   (The Duke in **Rigoletto**)

> *According to Gatti, Verdi found his very first crea-*
> *tions lacking in drama and variety: "Long experi-*
> *ence has confirmed the impression I have always*
> *had about dramatic effects, though in my first*
> *efforts I did not have the courage to express some*
> *of them. For example, ten years ago I would not*
> *have dared to set **Rigoletto** to music: today I would*
> *turn down subjects like Nabucco, Foscari, etc. While*
> *they are extremely interesting situations, they lack*
> *variety. They strike only one chord, a lofty one if*
> *you will, but always the same." (p. 124)*

Before examining verbs (which are by far the most important and complex of the nine parts of speech), brief mention should be made the **interjection** and the **conjunction**. Neither is difficult nor even very common, but a knowledge of both will help you decipher any libretto.

VII INTERJECTIONS

These are the short expressions which convey sudden emotion. In much the same way as the atmosphere-creating adjectives already discussed (pp. 33), interjections too set a certain tone, and Italian opera would certainly not be the same without them.

Some of the more common ones:

O ciel'!   (Heavens!)
Cospetto! (Bless me! What the blazes?! etc.)
Deh! (Alas, for pity's sake!)
Evviva! (Long live!...) "Evviva la Maga!"
   (Un Ballo in Maschera)
Guai! (Watch out! i. e. you're for it!)
Guai a te! ('You're in big trouble!)
Oimè! (Alas!): "Oimè, io piango!" (Alas, I weep!)
   (Rigoletto to the Courtiers)
Orsù! (Come on! 'Come off it!')
"Orsù, Tosca, parlate!"
(Come now, Tosca, speak!) (Scarpia to Tosca)
Per Bacco! (By Jove!, etc.)

Interjections are highly idiomatic and can only be approximated in translation. The best way to learn their nuances is to observe them in context. Mary McCarthy's **Florence** analyzes some of them.

VIII CONJUNCTIONS

These are the words which link other words, phrases and clauses. There are two kinds of conjunctions: co-ordinating and subordinating. Without putting too fine (and boring) a point on it, **co-ordinating conjunctions** join words of equal value. Typical ones are:

allora (so)	ma (but)
e (and)	ni (neither)
eppure (or)	però (but, however)

Example:

> (a) "Per sogni   e per chimere
> For dreams and for chimeras
> e per castelli   in aria,
> And for castles in the air,
> l'anima ho milionaria."
> I've a 'million dollar' soul.
> (Rodolfo to Mimi in **La Bohème**).

Subordinating conjunctions join clauses which can stand alone to those which cannot stand alone. They are difficult and will be dealt with in detail on pp. 108-9. Some typical subordinate conjunctions:

> perchè (because, in order that)   prima che (before)
> benchè (although)   se (if, unless)

Example:

> "S'io   non   tornassi, fate da   madre   a   Santa..."
> If I should not return   act as (a) mother to Santuzza.

-- "fate da madre a Santa" is an independent clause which makes sense on its own; "**io non tornassi**" only makes sense if accompanied by the conjunction "se", so it is a dependent clause. Clauses linked by subordinate conjunctions often have a complex relationship: hypothetical situations (which is the case in the example above), purpose, concessions, and the like. (Turiddu to his Mother in **Cavalleria Rusticana**). If this sounds like 'mumbo-jumbo' now, it will be clarified by the two chapters on the subjunctive mood... Not to worry!

This is really all you need to know about conjunctions. Now on to verbs, which are the most complicated part of speech and **the most important** key for unlocking the mysteries of the libretto.

Some lucky people don't seem to need books on operatic Italian because they learn all that they need to know effortlessly. Maria Callas is doubtless case in point, blessed with an ear for languages and an incredible memory. Recalling her childhood in New York City, she gives us a glimpse of this talent: "Elvira de Hidalgo used to lend me the full scores of operas which I could not have bought. I used to learn them off by heart, so as to give them back as soon as possible..." Some people have everything! (Quoted from Wisneski's "Maria Callas. The Art Behind the Legend.")

Maria Callas

CHAPTER FIVE

VERBS, PRESENT AND FUTURE

With the verb we come to the most important and complex part of speech in the libretto. A mastery of the verb, taken with what you know already about articles, nouns, prepositions, adjectives, adverbs, pronouns, interjections and conjunctions, should enable you to understand the greater part of a libretto. The next five chapters will tell you the essential about verbs. Then, armed with this knowledge and a good Italian-English dictionary (e.g., Hoare's, Collins'), containing a table of irregular verbs, you should be able to decipher almost anything.

There are two dimensions to every verb: **tense** i. e. **time** (horizontal in the outline below) and **mood** (vertical in the outline below). The table below shows a simplified outline of all the tenses and moods.

GIURARE (to swear an oath to, to promise)

MOOD / TIME	PAST	PRESENT	FUTURE
INDICATIVE	giurai (I swore)	giuro (I swear)	giurerò (I will swear)
IMPERATIVE	NIL	giura! (swear!)	NIL
SUBJUNCTIVE	ch'io giurassi (that I might have sworn)	ch'io giuri (that I might swear)	NIL (DOESN'T EXIST)

As you can see by reading the above table from **left to right**, a verb can be in only one tense at a time: the past, the present or the future. Similarly, reading the table from **top to bottom**, a verb can be in only one of three moods at a time: (1) the statement mood (or indicative); (2) the command mood (or imperative), and (3) the emotional/uncertainty mood (or subjunctive).

64

As a result, every verb has to fall into **one of the nine rectangles** (actually only six rectangles because some forms, e. g., the future subjunctive, simply do not exist) on the above table. For opera lovers the good news is that **opera tends to favor certain tenses** and to avoid many of the tenses common in modern Italian. As a result of this there are fewer for you to learn. In all of Aïda, for instance, there are only seven verb tenses. The not-so-good news is **that opera favors obsolete verb forms and difficult tenses** (especially the imperfect subjunctive) and that Italian has an enormous number of irregular i. e. unpredictable verbs.

In order to master verb tenses we will start with the indicative (Top of Table A) and procede to the **imperative** and the **subjunctive** (Bottom of Table A). The next five chapters have been laid out as follows: The current chapter covers the present, the future and the conditional of the indicative mood. **Chapter Six** outlines the essentials of the past indicative tenses (especially the simple past, the compound past, and the descriptive past). **Chapter Seven** deals with the imperative mood. **Chapters Eight** and **Nine** probe the complex subjunctive (present and imperfect). Throughout these chapters you will find **regular, irregular** and **reflexive** verbs.

By the end of Chapter Nine you should have enough knowledge to deal with most librettos. To round things off **Chapter Ten** explores any remaining grammar points which you need to know.

The first thing to know about verbs is that there are four main types or, as the grammarians put it, "conjugations":

lst conjugation	2nd conjug.	3rd conjug.	irregular
end in 'are'	end in 'ere'	end in 'ire'	unpredictable
parlare	**rispọndere**	**sentire** (to	**ẹssere**
(to speak)	(to reply)	hear, listen,	(to be)
		feel)	

DETAILED VERB TABLE (TABLE A)

| PAST TENSES | PRESENT TENSES | FUTURE TENSES |

A. STATEMENT MOOD

SIMPLE PAST (PRET.)   **PRESENT INDICATIVE/STATEMENT FUTURE**

io cantai (I sang)	io canto (I sing, etc.)	io canterò (I'll sing)
tu cantasti (you sang)	tu canti (you sing, etc.	tu canterai (you'll sing)
ei cantò (he sang)	ei canta (he's singing)	ei canterà (he'll sing)
noi cantammo (we sang)	cantiamo (we sing)	canteremo (we'll sing)
voi cantaste (you sang)	voi cantate (you sing)	canterete (you'll sing)
essi cantarono (they sang)	essi cantano (they sing)	canteranno (they'll sing)

COMPOUND PAST ('PRESENT PERFECT')   **CONDITIONAL**

io ho cantato (I have sung)	canterei (I would sing)
tu hai cantato (you have sung)	canteresti (you would sing)
ha cantato (s/he has sung)	canterebbe (he would sing)
abbiamo cantato (we have sung)	canteremmo (we wld. sing)
avete cantato (you have sung)	cantereste (you wld. sing)
hanno cantato (they have sung)	canterebbero (they'd sing)

DESCRIPTIVE PAST ('IMPERFECT')   **FUTURE PAST (RARE)**

io cantavo (I was singing, used to sing)	io avrò cantato (I shall
tu cantavi (you were singing, etc.)	have sung)
cantava (s/he was singing, etc.)	
cantavamo (we were singing, etc.)	
cantavate (you were singing, etc.)	
cantavano (they were singing, etc.)	

CANTARE, the 'infinitive' form, means 'to sing' e. g. vorrei cantare (I'd like to sing).
CANTANDO: singing e. g. stavo cantando (I was singing). CANTATO means 'sung'.

PAST TENSES	PRESENT TENSES	FUTURE TENSES

B. COMMAND (IMPERATIVE) MOOD

PAST TENSES	PRESENT TENSES	FUTURE TENSES
NO TENSES HERE BUT THE IMPERFECT SUB-JUNCTIVE (BELOW) IS USED TO FILL THE GAP.	ch'io *canti (Oh, let me sing!) canta! (sing!) ch'ei *canti! (Let him sing!) cantiamo! (Let's sing!) cantate! (sing!) ch'essi *cantino! (Let them sing!)	GOOD NEWS! NO TENSES HERE. THERE IS NO FUT. IMPERATIVE. As you can see from this Table, there are only three time frames for any verb: the past, the pres. and the future.

C. SUBJUNCTIVE (DOUBT, ETC.) MOOD

IMPERFECT SUBJUNCTIVE	PRESENT SUBJUNCTIVE	
ch'io cantassi (that I might have sung) che tu cantassi ch'ei cantasse che cantaste che cantassimo che cantassero	ch'io canti (that I might sing) che tu canti (that you ...) ch'essa canti (that she...) cha noi cantiamo che voi cantiate ch'essi cantino	There are also only three MOODS POSSIBLE: (statement), COMMAND (imperative) and SUB-JUNCTIVE (doubt/emotion) FOR THE TENSE READ ACROSS THE TABLE. FOR THE MOOD READ UP AND DOWN. NO FUTURE SUBJUNCTIVE.

* The three asterisked forms are borrowed from the present subjunctive

Regular verbs (first three conjugations) will follow a predictable pattern. All other verbs are more or less 'mavericks' and unpredictable. These are called "irregular" verbs and the only thing easy about them is that quite a few (**avere**, **essere**, **vedere**, etc.) are used so often that you become used to them. A good Italian-English dictionary will list a table of the most common irregular verbs, which is a help.

The first three conjugations are formed as follows in the **present indicative** (statement mood):

FIRST CONJUGATION
(are) e.g.,"scherzare": to joke, jest

io scherzo (I joke)   noi scherziamo (we are joking)
tu scherzi (you joke)   voi scherzate   (you are joking)
egli (he); essa (she) scherza   essi/esse scherzano
(he/she is joking, jokes, etc.)   (they are joking)

SECOND CONJUGATION
(ere) e.g.,"rispondere", to reply

io   rispondo   noi rispondiamo
tu   rispondi   voi rispondete
egli risponde   essi rispondono

THIRD CONJUGATION
(ire) e.g., "sentire", to feel, to listen

io   sento   noi sentiamo
tu   senti   voi sentite
essa sente   esse sentono

The grammar enthusiast will want to know that the present indicative is formed by taking the **"infinitive"** (i. e. the complete form of the verb—**scherzare** in the first conjugation), dropping its distinctive ending (**"are"** in this case) and adding the appropriate endings (o, i, a, etc.). You do not have to know this process in order to learn operatic (or modern) Italian, but some people learn languages easily via grammar; others are more like Maria Callas (see page 63) and seem to pick them up through some kind of osmosis. Whatever category you fall into, you will find it useful to familiarize yourself with the many operatic extracts which I have included.

Some typical extracts (present indicative):

(1) "Il tempo **incalza**" (from **incalzare**): 'time is pressing'. 3rd person singular.
(Manrico to the Messenger in **Il Trovatore**).

(2) "**Vagheggi** il regno d'altra beltà."
(from **vagheggiare**): 'You covet the reign of another beauty.' 2nd person singular.
(Iago to Cassio in **Otello**).

(3) "Per l'infelice patria,/ Per me...per voi **pavento**."
(from **paventare**): 'For the unhappy fatherland, For me... for you I fear.' 1st person singular.
(Aïda to Amneris).

(4) "Non **venite** alla messa?" (from **venire**)
'Aren't you coming to mass?' 2nd person plural (used here with the meaning of a singular).
(Lola to Santuzza in **Cavalleria Rusticana**)

(5) "A voi **pensiamo**, ô belle occhi-di-sole!"
(from **pensare**): 'Of you we think, oh beautiful eyes-of-sun.' 1st person plural.
(Chorus of farmers in **Cavalleria Rusticana**).

(6) "Abbandonata in questo/ Popoloso deserto Che **appelano** Parigi." (from **appelare**):
'Abandoned in this populous desert which they call Paris.' 3rd person plural.
(Violetta to herself in **La Traviata**).

(7) "Già **sorge** il sole." (from **sorgere**): 'Already the sun is rising.' 3rd pers. singular. (Tosca to herself).

(8) "Ô Dio, non **rispondi**!" (from **rispondere**)
'Oh, God, you don't reply!' 2nd person singular.
(Orfeo to Euridice)

Here are the present indicative forms of some of the more common **irregular verbs. Note the alternative archaic forms which are often favored by librettists.** For example, if you look at the forms of "dovere", you will see three ways of saying "I must": "Io devo", "Io deggio" and "Io debbo". All three are found in opera, but only "Io devo" is common in modern Italian.

avere (to have) io ho (I have)   noi abbiamo
                  tu hai   voi avete
                  ei ha   essi hanno
                                    ('h' is silent)

dovere (to be obligated to)
                  io devo/deggio/debbo noi dobbiamo
                  tu devi (dei)   voi dovete
                  ei deve (he must) essi devono
                                      /debbono

essere (to be)   io sono (I am)   noi siamo
                  tu sei   voi siete
                  egli è   esse sono

fare (to make, do, commit, etc.)
                  io faccio/fo (I do)   noi   facciamo
                  tu fai   voi   fate
                  ella fa   essi   fanno

potere (to be able)
                  io posso (I can)   noi   possiamo
                  tu puoi   voi   potete
                  egli può/puote   essi   possono
                                      /ponno

vedere (to see) io vedo/veggo/veggio noi vediamo
                  tu vedi (you see)   voi vedete
                  egli vede   essi vedono

And here is how they are used:

(1) "Benvenuto! Con noi **dovete** bere!" (from **dovere**): 'Welcome! With us you must drink!' 2nd person plural used in the sense of a formal singular. (Alfio to Turiddu in **Cavalleria Rusticana**)

(2) "Il mio universo è in te!" (from **essere**): 'My universe is in you!' 3rd person singular. (Rigoletto to Gilda)

REFLEXIVE VERBS

Before looking at the future tense, note that many verbs can take on a slightly different meaning when they are used with the reflexive pronoun (discussed on p. 55). If **"io chiamo"** means 'I call', **"io mi chiamo"** means "I call myself" i. e. "My name is...". (In the plural, **a reciprocal meaning** is gained through the reflexive: **"si amano"** means **"they love each other"**.) It is vital to be able to recognize reflexive verbs because **they are used much more in Italian** (operatic or otherwise) **than they are in English**. From here on I will include reflexive verbs with non-reflexive verbs in dealing with the various tenses and moods.

To form the reflexive verb a reflexive pronoun is added to the verb. "Io muto" means 'I change'; but **io** (subject pronoun) **mi** (reflexive pronoun) **muto** (verb)" i. e. **"io mi muto"** means "I transform myself". The complete picture is as follows:

mi muto (I transform myself)   ci mutiamo
                                 (we transform ourselves)
ti muti (you transform yourself)   vi mutate (you transform
                                 yourself/yourselves)
si muta   (she/he/it transforms   si mutano (they transform
            herself/himself/itself)   themselves)

In **Il Trovatore** you find the very strange lines:

In upupa   o   strige
Into hoopoe (a kind of bird) or screech-owl
Talor'   **si muta.**
Sometimes   she transforms herself.

Sometimes she (Azucena's dead mother, who was burnt at the stake) changes into a bird (significantly a predator...). "Si muta" here is a reflexive, conveying the sense that the old witch deliberately assumes frightening forms. (Note the concision , referred to earlier, of certain operatic phrases such as "Talor' si muta"). "Mutare" without the reflexive pronoun has quite a different meaning, as in the Duke's famous lines:

La donna è   mobile,   qual' piuma   al vento.
'The' lady is   changeable, like (a) feather in the wind.
Muta   d'accento   e di pensiero.
She changes 'language' and   thought.

Here is another reflexive from the Duke in the aria 'Questa o Quella':

(1) "Sol'   chi vuole   **si   serbi**   fedele!"
   Only he who wants to, let him keep himself   faithful!
   —"si serbi": present (subjunctive), 3rd person singular, of
      serbarsi, to preserve/keep oneself, etc.

The plot thickens: in Italian there exists a large group of verbs which are reflexive **in form** but which **do not have a real reflexive meaning**. Such verbs translate quite differently from the true reflexives and their real meaning is often rather unpredictable:

(1) "Masetto, guarda ben',   **ti pentirai!**"
     Masetto, watch well (watch out), you will regret it!
     —"ti **pentirai**": future, 2nd person singular, of
        pentirsi, to repent oneself of, i. e. regret. The
        form is reflexive, but the verb itself has a non-
        reflexive meaning.
        (Don Giovanni to Masetto in **Don Giovanni**).

(2) "Quand'ei **s'accorse** della vendetta/Restò scornato
     ad imprecar'!"
     (When he became aware of the vengeance / He re-
     mained i.e.'was left' humiliated, to curse!)
     —"s'accorse": preterite (simple past), 3rd person
        singular, of **accorgersi**, to become aware of, to
        notice, to realize, etc.
        (The Courtiers describing Rigoletto to the Duke).

If you look at the verb outline (pp. 66-7) you will see that you now know all about the present indicative tense and are ready to deal with the future indicative.

THE FUTURE INDICATIVE

It was observed earlier (p. 40) that certain adjectives contain the essence of the opera in which they are found. The same can be said of verb tenses, which are often the hallmark of a character and do much to develop him/her psychologically. It is fitting that Don Giovanni, a bully who revels in power, should use the 'command mood', (the imperative) so often. Similarly, in **Il Barbiere**, Rosina's determination to escape from Bartolo and marry Lindoro is admirably conveyed by the future tense. Tosca's use of the preterite in 'Vissi d'Arte' suggests the passionate intensity with which she lived and by its finality even hints at her impending doom. Carlo's nagging doubts about Alvaro's identity in **La Forza del Destino** takes the grammatical form of an imperfect subjunctive ("S'ei fosse il seduttore!?": 'What if' he were the seducer!?') And so on. Verbs help to develop theme and character.

It is not surprising that opera, which is the realm of determination, heroic resolve, vengeance, Machiavellian plotting, etc. should use the future so often. Manrico in **Il Trovatore** is a good case in point:

> "Empii,   spegnetelo,   o ch'io tra poco
> Impious ones, extinguish it (the fire) or I   shortly
> col vostro   sangue lo   **spegnerò!**"
> with your   blood   it   I will extinguish!
> —"spegnerò": future tense of **spegnere**, to extinguish.

If you prefer the "nuts and bolts" (grammar!) approach, the future indicative tense is formed by taking the 'stem' (which is usually very much like the 'infinitive' of the verb minus the final 'e': 'risponder', 'sentir', etc.) and adding the future endings: "ò", [ɔ] "ai", "à", etc. In the case of 'scherzare', the stem is 'scherzer', and the endings ò, ai, etc. (io scherzerò: I will joke) as shown below:

io scherzerò (I will joke)   noi scherzeremo (we will joke)
tu scherzerai (you will joke)   voi scherzerete (you will joke)
egli, ella scherzerà (he/she   essi/esse scherzeranno (they will
                will joke)   joke)

Typical verbs in the future indicative (statement mode):

SECOND CONJUGATION (rispondere)		THIRD CONJUGATION (punire)	
(io) risponderò	risponderemo	(io) punirò	puniremo
risponderai	risponderete	punirai	punirete
risponderà	risponderanno	punirà	puniranno

Some typical extracts with the future indicative (regular verbs):

1. "...e là,   gioiello mio,   **ci   sposeremo.**"
   'and there, my jewel,   we will get married.'
   —"sposeremo": from **sposare**, to marry,
   1st conjugation, 1st person plural.
   Note the reciprocal action in "ci sposeremo".
   (Don Giovanni to Zerlina in **Don Giovanni**).

2. "Mi **coglierà** sventura? Ah, no! E (è) follia!"
   Me will seize misfortune? Oh, no! It's folly!
   Will misfortune seize me?
   (from **cogliere**, to seize, 3rd person singular.
   Rigoletto to himself in 'Cortigiani, Vil' Razza
   Dannata!')

3. "(...) in eterno, per voi   **pregherò.**"
   Eternally,   for you   I shall pray.
   (from **pregare**, to pray).
   1st person singular (Gilda to Rigoletto)

Irregular verbs have **their own future stem**, which often looks nothing like the infinitive:

avere (to have)	Future stem: **avr**	io avrò	(I will have)
essere (to be)	Future stem: **sar**	io sarò	(I will be)
fare (to do, etc.)	Future stem: **far**	io farò	(I will do)
potere (to be able)	Future stem: **potr**	io potrò	(I will be able to)
sapere (to know)	Future stem: **sapr**	io saprò	(I will know)
venire (to come)	Future stem: **verr**	io verrò	(I will come)

74

Some typical extracts of the future indicative of irregular verbs:

1. "Là   ci   **darem'**   la mano."
   There   to each other we'll give the hand.
   1st person plural of **darsi** (a reflexive: to give
   to oneself, etc.)   (Don Giovanni to Zerlina).

2. "Là   mi   **dirai**   di   sì."
   There to me   you will   say   'yes'.
   2nd person singular of **dire** (to say)
   (Don Giovanni to Zerlina).

3. "Ma   ne   **avrò**   vendetta."
   But   'for it'   I will have vengeance.
   1st person singular of **avere** (to have)
   (The Duke to himself in **Rigoletto**).

4. "(...) te colpire   il   buffone   **saprà**."
   ...to strike you   the buffoon   will know how to
   3rd person singular of **sapere** (to know how to, etc.)
   (Rigoletto to the Duke's portrait)

5. "Vi   **farete**   criticar'."
   You will make yourself   criticized
   2nd person plural (used as a singular) of **fare**
   (to do, make, etc.)
   (Don Giovanni to Donna Elvira)

6. "Che **farò**   senza di te,   Euridice?"
   What will I do   without you,   Euridice?
   1st person singular. (Orfeo to Euridice).

There are also some tricky obsolete forms of the future. "**Essere**" (to be), for instance, has three future forms, two of which are very irregular and not used in modern Italian: "**fora**" and "**fia**" (both 3rd person singular). They are quite common. Examples:

1. "...questa   man' per   voi   **fora**   cruenta."
   this   hand for   you   will be cruel.
   3rd person singular of **essere** (to be).
   (Rigoletto to the Courtiers).

2. "Sotto il mio ciel' più libero
   Under my sky more free
   L'amor' ne **fia** concesso."
   Love to us will be granted.
   3rd person singular of **essere** (to be).
   (Aïda to Radamès.)

Rosina's famous cavatina in **Il Barbiere** shows how well the repetition of the future tense conveys determination.

1. Una voce poco fa... (...)
   A voice a little while ago (...)
2. Sì, Lindoro mio **sarà.** (future of **essere**)
   Yes, Lindoro mine will be.
3. Lo giurai, la **vincerò.** (future of **vincere**)
   I swore it, it I shall win.
4. Il tutor' **ricuserà.** (future of **ricusare**)
   The tutor (Bartolo) he (Lindoro) will stand up to.
5. Io l'ingegno **aguzzerò.** (fut. of **aguzzare**)
   'my' mind I will sharpen.
6. Alla fin' **s'accheterà.** (fut. of **acchetarsi**)
   In the end he (Bartolo) will be silent.
7. E contenta io **resterò.** (fut. of **restare**)
   And content I shall remain.
8. Sì, Lindoro mio **sarà.** (fut. of **essere**)
   Yes, Lindoro mine shall be.

All of the present indicative and future indicative verbs in Butterfly's famous aria have been printed with their infinitives in parentheses. See how many of the forms you can translate and identify. The first sentence has been done for you. As usual, the answers can be found in Chapter Twelve.

76

UN BEL DI VEDREMO

1. Senti— Un bel dì **vedremo** (from **vedere**, to see)
   Listen— One fine day (we will see: fut.,1st pers.plural)
   VERB ART ADJ. NOUN VERB

2. levarsi un fil' di fumo sull' estremo
   'raise itself'[1] a thread of smoke on the extreme
   VERB ART. NOUN PREP. NOUN PREP./ART ADJ.

3. confin' del mare.
   edge of the sea.
   NOUN PREP./ART. NOUN

4. E poi la nave appare (from **apparire**)
   And then the ship appears
   CONJ. ADV. ART. NOUN VERB

5. E poi la nave è (from **essere**, to be) bianca.
   And then the ship _____ white.
   CONJ. ADV. ART. NOUN VERB ADJ.

6. **Entra** (from **entrare**) nel porto;
   _____ into (the) port;
   VERB PREP./ART. NOUN

7. **Romba** (from **rombare**, to boom out) il suo saluto.
   _____ its greeting.
   VERB ART. ADJ. NOUN

8. **Vedi?** (**vedere**, to see) E (è) venuto! (past tense of **venire**)
   _____ He (Pinkerton) has come!
   VERB VERB

---

[1] Throughout this book I have used inverted commas to indicate that I have had to paraphrase: (a) because of a gap ('lacuna' in technical English) or (b) because I have been forced to use unidiomatic English in order to capture the essence of the Italian. (Verse 2 is a case of the latter.)

9. Io   non gli   **scendo (scendere,** descend) incontro, io no:
   I   don't 'for him' _____ towards, not I:
   PRO. PRO. (DAT. OF ADV.)   VERB   PREP.   PRON.

10. **Mi metto (mettersi)** là sul   ciglio   del   colle
    _____ there on the 'eyelash' of the hill
    VERB   ADV. PR.ART. NOUN   PR./ART. NOUN

11. E **aspetto (aspettare,** wait), e   aspetto per gran tempo
    And _____   and _____ for a long time
    CONJ. VERB   CONJ. VERB PREP. ADJ. NOUN

12. E   non mi   **pesa (pesare,** to weigh on,etc.) la lunga attesa.
    And _____ the long wait.
    CONJ. PRON. (DAT.OF ADV.)   VERB   ART.ADJ. NOUN

13. E,   uscito   dalla   folla cittadina un   uomo,
    And, 'emerged' from the   city crowd   a   man,
    CONJ. VERB   PREP./ART. NOUN ADJ.   ART. NOUN

14. un   picciol' punto **s'avvia (avviarsi,** to make one's way)
    a   little   speck _____
    ART.   ADJ.   NOUN

15. per   la   collina.
    towards the   hill.
    PREP.   ART.   NOUN

16. Chi   **sarà? (essere,** to be) Chi   **sarà?**
    Who _____?   Who _____?
    PRON. VERB   PRON.   VERB

17. E   come   **sarà giunto** (from **giungere,** to arrive)
    And   when   he'will have arrived' ('future past tense')
    CONJ. ADV.   VERB

18. che   **dirà** (from **dire,** to say)?   Che   **dirà?**
    what _____ ?   What _____?
    PRON. VERB   PRON. VERB

78

19. **Chiamerà (chiamare, to call)** Butterfly dalla lontana.
_____ Butterfly 'from the distance',
VERB NOUN PREP./ ART. NOUN

20. Io senza dar' risposta,
I without giving reply,
PRON. PREP. VERB NOUN

21. **me ne starò** (from **starsene**, to remain) nascosta,
_____ hidden,
VERB (REFLEXIVE) ADJECTIVE

22. un po' per celia, e un po' per non morir(e)
a little through modesty, and a little in order not to die
ART. NOUN PREP. NOUN CONJ. ART./NOUN PREP. VERB

23. al primo incontro.
at the first encounter.
PREP./ART. ADJ. NOUN

24. Ed egli alquanto in pena **chiamerà (chiamare)**, chiamerà:
And he a little in pain _____ _____:
CONJ./PRON .ADV. PREP. NOUN VERB VERB

25. "Piccina mogliettina,
Little "nice little wife",
ADJ. NOUN

26. Olezzo di verbena."
Scent of verbena.
NOUN PREP. NOUN

27. ...i nomi che mi dava al suo venire.
the names that to me he gave at his (first) coming.
ART. NOUN CONJ. PRON. PRON. VERB PREP./ART. ADJ. NOUN (VB)

28. Tutto questo **avverrà** (from **avvenire**, to come to pass),
All this _____,
ADJ. PRON. VERB

29.te   lo   **prometto** (from **promettere**, to promise).

to you it   _____.

PRON. PRON.   VERB

30.**Tienti** (refl.'command' tense of **tenere**, to hold) la tua paura.

Keep for yourself i. e. 'hold in', control   your fear.

VERB PRON.   ART. ADJ. NOUN

31. Io   con   sicura   fede   **l'aspetto.**

I   with   certain   faith   _____him.

PRON. PREP. ADJ.   NOUN   PRON. VERB.

Tebaldi singing 'Un Bel Dì' from **Madame Butterfly**.
(The Lyric Opera of Chicago).

CONDITIONAL (INDICATIVE) TENSE

The conditional tense is a cousin to the future but it conveys the idea of a condition or a wish. Take **cantare**, to sing. The future tense is **io canterò** (I will sing, I shall sing), which is forceful and determined. The conditional tense is **io canterei** (I would sing, I will sing if conditions permit, etc.) which is not as forceful. As you can see from the following outline, the conditional uses the same stem (**canter**) as the future, but adds different endings to it.

The regular forms:

(io) canterei (I would sing)	canteremmo (we would sing)
(tu) canteresti (you would sing)	cantereste (you would sing)
(ei) canterebbe (he would sing)	canterebbero (they would sing)

One oddity of the conditional is the alternative old-fashioned form (**ia**) which is found only in the first and third persons:

(io)   canteria (I would sing)
(essa) canteria (she would sing) essi canterian (they would sing)

These forms are quite common in opera; the following are typical:

1. "Ei che **vorria** dell'anima / Farti quaggiù   beata."
   He who would like with (his) soul to make you 'here below'
   blessed. **Vorria** is the alternative conditional of **volere**, to want/desire.
   (The Duke to Gilda in **Rigoletto**).
   An interesting satanic use of religious language with seductive intent.

2. "Dirlo ad altri   ei **potria** (from **potere**, to be able)
   To say it (to another) he would be capable

   Nè   sventura   per me certo   **saria** (from **essere**)."
   Neither misfortune for me   certainly it would (not) be.
   Certainly for me it wouldn't be a misfortune.
   (The Duke to the Courtiers in **Rigoletto**).

Here are some typical extracts showing both forms of the conditional:

1. "Il tuo bel   cielo **vorrei** (from **volere**, to desire) ridarti..."
   your beautiful sky   I would like to   give back to you.
   (Radamès to himself in 'Celeste Aïda'.)

2. "Chi scoprirlo **potria**?" (from **potere**, to be capable of, etc.)
   Who to discover it would be able? (Aïda to Amonasro)

3. "Prode t'amai,   non   **t'amerei**   spergiuro.
   Brave   I loved you, I wouldn't love you (if you were) false
   i. e. untrue to your word. (Aïda to Radamès.)

4. "Abbandonarmi   così **potresti** (from **potere**)?"
   To abandon me   thus   you would be able?
   (Pollione to Adalgisa in **Norma**)

5. "**Potrian**' seguirla,   rapirla   ancora!"
   They could follow her,   (and) abduct her still!
   (Rigoletto to himself)

6. "Io   **darei** (from **dare**, to give) la   vita
   I   would give   'my' life

   per   asciugar' quel   pianto!"
   to   dry   'those   tears' (lit. 'that crying')
   (Scarpia in **Tosca**.)

7. "Signor' nè   principe io lo **vorrei** (from **volere**, to wish)
   (Neither) lord nor prince   I would wish him

   Sento che   povero più **l'amerei**" (from **amare**)
   I feel that (if he were) poor, more I would love him.
   (Gilda to Giovanna in **Rigoletto**.)
   Note the concision of the original.

82

"I should like nothing better than to find a good libretto as well as a good poet (...). It is impossible, or almost impossible , for anyone else to know what it is I want. I want subjects that are new, great, beautiful, varied, strong (...) with new forms, etc.,etc. and at the same time suitable for music."
(Letter of Jan. 1, 1853. Verdi *to Cesare de Sanctis. See* **"Letters of Giuseppe Verdi"**, *p. 89)*

Richard Tucker as the Duke of Mantua, Ettore Bastianini as Rigoletto in 1962 (The Lyric Opera of Chicago).

CHAPTER SIX

THE PAST INDICATIVE TENSES

As shown by the Table (p.66), in opera there are three main past tenses used in the indicative (statement) mood[1] Taking "cantare" as a model, these three tenses are:

(1) **"cantai"** (I sang) This is the **simple past** (more formally called the preterite).

(2) **"ho cantato"** (I have sung, etc.). In order to avoid confusion I shall refer to it as the **"compound past"**. Its traditional name, the "present perfect", does not describe it well.

(3) **"cantavo"** (I used to sing, I was singing at that time, etc.). This is best referred to as the **"descriptive past"** tense. Its traditional name, the "imperfect", does not clarify its meaning much. From this point on **I will use my terms instead of the more traditional ones** (which have done much to turn many people off grammar...).

The simple past and the compound past convey action for the most part and are used interchangeably. The key difference is that the simple past has concision, vigor, elegance, and a literary quality—characteristics which are lacking in the compound past. **In opera the simple past is used to an extraordinary degree,** much more than the compound past. This is not surprising, considering what we know about composers' and librettists' penchant for the rare, the unusual and the esoteric. The descriptive past describes a situation or conveys the idea of habitual action. Such is the overview. Now for the details. First, the simple past.

---

[1] There are a few others, but they are not common: (a) the pluperfect, e.g., "I avevo cantato" (I had sung). Pluperfect reflexives are also found from time to time, e. g., 'si era previsto' (from **prevedersi**, to foresee), meaning 'it had been foreseen'. Such tenses are rare, however, and deserve no more than a footnote.

THE SIMPLE PAST (PRETERITE)

FIRST CONJUGATION (ARE) "pugnare", to fight.

io pugnai   (I fought)   noi pugnammo (we fought)
tu pugnasti (you fought)   voi pugnaste   (you fought)
pugnò (he/she/it fought)   pugnarono   (they fought)

Note that the third person plural is sometimes shortened to "pugnaro".

SECOND CONJUGATION (ERE)
"ricevere", to receive.

io ricevei (I received)   noi ricevemmo (we received)
ricevesti (you received)   riceveste (you received)
ricevè (he/she/it received)   riceverono (they received)

THIRD CONJUGATION (IRE)
"partire", to leave.

io partii (I left)   noi partimmo (we left)
partisti (you left)   partiste (you left)
partì (he/she/it) left   partirono (they left)

Typical examples:

(1)"Lo   **giurai**,   la vincerò!"
    I   swore it, I will win out!
   —"giurai": from **giurare**, to swear, i. e. to take an oath.
   lst person singular. (Rosina to herself in **Il Barbiere**.)

(2)"Frate! Troppo   **soffrii** il   tuo   parlar' crudel'!"
   Brother! Too long have I endured your cruel   speech!
   —"soffrii": from **soffrire**, to suffer, endure, put up with.
   lst person singular.
   (Filippo to the Grand Inquisitor in **Don Carlo**.)

(3) "Il sonno, ô Dio, **sparì** dai miei occhi languenti!"
Sleep, Oh God, disappeared from my languid eyes!
—"sparì": from **sparire**, to disappear. 3rd person singular.
Filippo to himself in **Don Carlo** ('Ella Giammai m'amò!')

(4) "E noi, clementi invero, **perdonammo!**"
And we, kind indeed, pardoned!
—"perdonammo": from **perdonare**, to pardon.
lst person plural.
(Rigoletto to the Duke and/or Monterone, in **Rigoletto.**)

(5) "Per qual' prezzo **vendeste** il mio bene?"
For what price did you sell my 'treasure' (i.e. Gilda)?
—"vendeste": from **vendere**, to sell.
(Rigoletto to the Courtiers.)

(6) "I vostri birri **frugaro** invan' tutta la villa."
Your 'flatfeet' searched in vain the whole villa.
—"frugaro": short (alternative) simple past of **frugare**,
to search intensively. ("Frugarono" would be the usual form.)
(Cavaradossi to Scarpia in **Tosca.**)

Irregular verbs abound in the simple past and since they are often quite different from what you might expect, they take some getting used to. Some common ones:

INFINITIVE	MEANING	PRETERITE FORMS
avere	to have	(io) ebbi, tu avesti, ei ebbe noi avemmo, voi aveste, essi ebbero

"Di lei contezza non **ebbi.**"
Of her (Leonora) news I didn't have.
(The Count in **Trovatore**)

essere	to be	(io) fui, tu fosti, ei fu, noi fummo, voi foste, ei furono

86

INFINIT.   MEANING   PRETERITE FORMS

Avere and **essere** are very common, but there are many others:

dare	to give	(io) diedi/detti, tu desti, ei diede, noi demmo, voi deste, ei diedero/dettero.
fare	to make, do, accomplish, etc.	(io) feci, tu facesti, ei fece, noi facemmo, voi faceste, ei fecero
tenere	to hold	(io) tenni, tu tenisti, ei tenne, noi tenemmo, voi teneste, ei tennero
vedere	to see	(io) vidi, tu vedesti, ei vide, noi vedemmo, voi vedeste, essi videro
vivere	to live	(io) vissi, vivesti, visse, vivemmo, viveste, vissero.
fare	to make, do, commit, etc.	(io) feci, facesti, fece, facemmo, faceste, fecero.
vedere	to see	(io) vidi, vedesti, vide, vedemmo, vedeste, videro.

Others: **pingere** (to paint): io **pinsi**; **scrivere** (to write): io **scrissi**; **tacere** (to remain silent): io **tacqui**; **venire** (to come): io **venni**.

Here are some irregular simple pasts in context:

(1) "L'orgoglio immenso **fu, fu** l'error' suo profondo!"
Immense   pride   it was; it was his   profound error!
—"fu": simple past of **essere**, to be. 3rd person singular.
(A Friar to his fellow monks in **Don Carlo.**)

(2) "Vil' scellerato   mi   **faceste**   voi!"
Vile villain   me   have made you
(A) vile   villain   you   (courtiers) have made me.
—"faceste": simple past of **fare**, to make, do, create, etc.
2nd person plural. Rigoletto to himself
('Cortigiani, Vil' Razza...')

87

(3) "Ô   gioia ch'io non   **conobbi,** ẹsser(e) amata amando!"
Oh joy that I have not   known: to be loved while loving in
—"conobbi": simple past of **conọscere:**   /return.
to know, to experience. 1st person singular.
(Violetta to herself in **La Traviata.**)

(4) "(1) Giusto (4) quei petti   (2) sdegno (3) **commosse;**
Righteous   those chests   indignation   moved;
(Righteous indignation moved those chests i. e. 'hearts'.)
—"commosse": simple past of **commuọvere,** to move.
3rd person singular. Note the twisted structure of this one!

L'insana   vẹcchia   lo **provocò!**"
The insane old woman provoked it!
—"provocọ̀": simple past of **provocare,** to provoke.
3rd person singular. (The Count's retainers in **Il Trovatore.**)

(5) "Caro nome che il mio cor'/ **Festi**   prima   palpitạr'..."
Dear   name which my heart/ Made 'throb' for the first time.
—"festi": simple past of **fare,** to make, etc.
2nd person singular.   Note the alternative archaic form.
Gilda to herself in **Rigoletto** ('Caro Nome').

HOW TO UNRAVEL A LIBRETTO
(THE REDUCTIVE PROCESS)

The quickest way to learn to recognize difficult verb tenses like
the irregular simple past is through a reductive process. By now you
can recognize the subject (usually a noun or a pronoun), and other
parts of speech (articles, prepositions, adjectives, adverbs, interjections and conjunctions). One you have identified these, the difficult
missing link will often be an irregular verb (which you can look up
in a good English-Italian dictionary).

For example, if you came across this verse of Amneris from
Aïda:

"Sacerdoti, compiste un diletto!"

you know enough by now to identify "sacerdoti" and "diletto" as
nouns. You might even have a good idea as to their meaning

("sacerdoti" means priests; "diletto" means crime). Through reductive logic, "compiste" has to be a verb. But which verb? And which tense? From the context (Amneris berating Ramfis and the other priests for the unfair death sentence which they have meted out to Radamès) you know that the verb has a negative ring to it and this information will help you to choose the right verb when you look it up in the verb table amongst those infinitives which start with the same four letters. "Compiere" is the infinitive which you want and, sure enough, when you look at its preterite forms (most of which will be listed), you will find "compiste". This might seem like a lot of work, but (and this is probably true of learning any language), the sooner you can get by without translations (and those very distracting surtitles which have been in vogue for the past few years),[2] the sooner you will have the satisfaction of perceiving directly with all your senses the intensity of the original libretto so that you can **savour the visual aspects of the operatic spectacle itself**. As I mentioned earlier, the process is immensely satisfying and there is nothing quite like it. I think that any true opera lover should consider making the effort, no matter what the language: Italian, German, French, or Russian. As for myself, I look forward some day to learning enough German to do Wagner justice.

> *There are evidently many people (...) who in the first instance picked up foreign languages by working at opera librettos, notably those literal translations that came with the (Mozart Opera Society) albums. The range of communication which is possible through tags, mainly operatic, is fairly large. One can astonish the sleepy occupants of the Orient Express by exclaiming (with Tamino),'O ew'ge*

[2] Surtitles (or, on television, subtitles) can help the audience to appreciate the original Italian and they are much better than nothing (or striking matches to read a libretto in the dark...) but of course they can never be as satisfying as being able to understand the original. They can also be very distracting, drawing the viewer's eye from the action on the stage to a line of print. It is difficult to have one eye on the pot and the other up the chimney... Nevertheless, once you master librettos you will enjoy finding errors in the surtitles, I suppose. It will be a rather sad day for opera when opera-goers watch the screen more than the stage (which I actually saw happen at a production of Aïda at the Colosseum in Vancouver in 1989).

Nacht, wann wirst du schwinden?' Italian hotels
understand a scribbled instruction, 'Ah! non mi
ridestar'!' pinned to the door.
(from "The Opera Bedside Book", p. 211 ff.)

To return to irregular simple pasts, if you follow the reductive process above, you will not only become familiar with the difficult forms, but also you will acquire subtler benefits such as the ability to make associations, for example, once you know "compiere", when you hear it in **Aïda** you will automatically think of how it is used to advantage in other contexts as well; it has its place of honor, for instance, in that glorious ringing verse sung by the Druids as they announce Norma's entrance:

"I suoi riti a **compiere**, Norma (...) dal tempio   move".
her   rites to carry out Norma from the temple 'is coming'.
Norma is coming from the temple to carry out her rites.

When you can make such connections you will be well on your way to feeling and understanding Italian opera in depth, without clumsy, inaccurate translations. You will even be a bit like Verdi thinking of Bellini. These are joyous, pleasurable experiences.

Before moving on to the other two indicative tenses (the compound past and the descriptive past), let's have a look at "Vissi d'Arte", and see how effectively Puccini (and Giacosa and Illica, his librettists) use the simple past to poignantly sum up her life. It is just the right tense here—the tense of epitaphs.

1. **Vissi** d'arte,   **vissi** d'amore; (simple past of **vivere**)
   I lived 'on' art,   I lived 'on' love;

2. Non **feci** mai male   ad   anima viva! (from **fare**)
   I never did harm (evil) to   (a) living soul!

3. Con man(o) furtiva   quante miserie **conobbi**, **alleviai**.
   With (a) hand furtive   as many sufferings as I learned of,
   I assuaged.
   —"conobbi" comes from **conoscere**: to know, to learn of, etc.
   —"alleviai" comes from **alleviare**: to alleviate, assuage, etc

90

4. Sempre   con   fè   sincera
   Always   with   faith   sincere

5. la mia preghiera   ai   santi tabernacoli **salì**!
   my prayer   at the holy altars   'took flight'!
   —"salì" comes from **salire**: to rise, go up, ascend, etc.

6. **Diedi** fiori   agli altari, **diedi**   gioielli della Madonna
   al manto. (I gave flowers to the altars, gave jewels to the
   cape of the Madonna.)
   —"diedi" comes from **dare**, to give.

7. e   **diedi**   il canto   agli   astri,   al   ciel(o),
   and I gave   song   to the   stars, to the   sky/Heaven,

8. che   ne   ridean(o)[3]   più   belli.
   which for it (this action) 'emerged'   more   beautiful.

9. Nell'ora   del   dolor',   perchè,   Signore,
   In the hour of   grief,   why,   Lord,

10. perchè   me ne remuneri   così?
    why   do you repay   me for   it thus?

The melody is simple, majestic, grandiose, poignant—call it
what you will, but the libretto here is anything but simple; on the
contrary, it is compact and convoluted in the extreme. Archaic
expressions compound the difficulty. Taken together, the melody
and the words form an entity which does not yield the full force of
its magic easily. It should be noted in passing that the simple past
has a peculiarly sophisticated Tuscan feel to it (and in fact only in
Tuscany will you hear this literary tense even in the market place!)
and sits particularly well in the music of Puccini, himself a Tuscan
from Lucca.

---

[3] "ridean(o)" is an alternative imperfect of **redire**, an obsolete verb meaning to
return and, by extension, to emerge. More simply, it could come from **ridere**, to
laugh: 'The stars laughed, etc.'

THE COMPOUND PAST TENSE (INDICATIVE)

The compound past tense is used pretty well interchangeably with the simple past and it would serve no purpose to even attempt to explain where each is used. Nevertheless, it can safely be said of librettists that they prefer the simple past to the compound past tense because the latter is not as literary and formal in style and is therefore not as well suited to elevated, tragic subjects like **Norma**, **Lucia**, **Rigoletto**, and so on.

The compound past tense (or 'present perfect'—or 'passé composé' in French) is far easier to recognize than the simple past because, unlike the simple past, it always is accompanied by a 'helping verb' (**avere** or **essere**). As in French, the helping verb tends to be "essere" with verbs of motion and reflexives but "avere" with all other verbs.

Take "pugnare" (to fight). It logically takes "avere" as a helping verb; "andare" (to go) logically takes "essere" as a helping verb. Their complete forms are as follows:

PUGNARE

ho pugnato   (I have fought) abbiamo pugnato (we have fought)
hai pugnato (you have fought) avete pugnato (you have fought)
ha pugnato(she/he has fought) hanno pugnato   (they've fought)
(Don't forget that the "h" is silent in Italian.)

ANDARE

(io) sono andato/a (I have gone)   siamo andati/e (we have gone)
sei andato/a   (you have gone)   siete andati/e (you have gone)
è andato/a   (he/she has gone)   sono andati/e (they have gone)

As in French, the past participle (andato, etc.) will agree with the subject when "essere" is the helping verb (e. g., see extract three below: "Siam' giunti"). The past participle will also agree with the subject of a reflexive verb: "Essi si sono trasformati." (They have transformed themselves i. e. changed).

But enough grammar already! The following extracts will show you how the compound past is used:

(1) "Dimmi tu dove   l'hanno   nascosta."
    Tell me   where   they have   hidden her (Gilda).
    —"nascosta" is the past participle of **nascondere**: to hide.
    (Rigoletto to Marullo.)

(2) "Credo in un Dio crudel' che m'**ha creato** simile a sè!"
    I believe in a God cruel   who has made me similar to
    (Iago to himself in **Otello**).   himself.

(3) "**Siam' giunti**;   ecco la   torre
    We have arrived;   behold the   tower
    —"giunti" comes from **giungere**: to reach (a destination), etc.

    Ove   di   stato gemono   i   prigionieri..."
    Where (of the) state   groan i.e. suffer   the prisoners.
    (Ruiz to Leonora in **Il Trovatore**).

(4) "**Perduto   ha   la   gobba?**"
    Has he lost   the   hump?
    —"perduto" is the past participle of **perdere**: to lose.
    (The Courtiers to Marullo in **Rigoletto**).

(5) "Dirti: per te   ho   pugnato,
    To tell you: for   you   I have fought,
    —"pugnato" is from **pugnare**.
    Per te   ho   vinto!"
    For you I have conquered!
    —"vinto" is the past participle of **vincere**: to defeat,
        to conquer.
    (Radamès to himself in 'Celeste Aïda').

THE PAST DESCRIPTIVE TENSE

If the simple past and the compound past are generally used to describe one action, the 'imperfect' is used to describe a situation which once existed or to refer to something which happened often. It is therefore more fitting to refer to this tense as the "**past descriptive**". It is the tense of Mario Cavaradossi in 'E Lucevan' le Stelle', in which Mario conjures up the fragile beauty of freedom and the time he shared with Tosca:

"E   **lucevan'**   le stelle,
And were shining the stars,
—"lucevano" is the 'past descriptive' of **lucere**:
   to shine, gleam.

Ed   **olezzava**   la terra...
And gave off a fragrance   the earth...
—"olezzava" is the past descriptive of **olezzare**:
   to 'fill with perfume'.

Unlike the (irregular) simple past, the past descriptive is easy to recognize. The imperfect of **lasciare** (to leave):

(io) lasciavo (I was leaving)   lasciavamo (we were leaving)
(tu) lasciavi (you were leaving) lasciavate (you were leaving)
ei lasciava (he was leaving)   lasciavano (they were leaving)

While the forms of the past descriptive are easy to recognize, the tense itself is not easy to translate. It has many nuances, depending on context, and familiarity with it in actual librettos is probably the only way to learn it. As with certain other tenses, the past descriptive has its rare, archaic forms. Once you know what to look for, however, this poses no problem. The following table shows the two forms (the 'normal' and the archaic) of the past descriptive:

INFINITIVE	MEANING	USUAL FORM[4]	ARCHAIC (OPERATIC)
avere	to have	io avevo	io avea
godere	to enjoy	io godevo	io godea
giungere	to arrive	io giungevo	io giungea
pascere	to feed on	io pascevo	io pascea
vedere	to see	io vedevo	io vedea

To complicate matters, in opera the past descriptive is occasionally used in exactly the same way as the simple past or the compound past i. e. it can sum up a situation:

"Nè **udivi** (2nd pers. sing. of **udire**, to hear) mai novella?"
did you hear   never news?
i.e. (Did you never hear news from him?)
(The Count to Azucena in **Il Trovatore**).

Just as Tosca sums up her life in 'Vissi d'Arte', Mario Cavaradossi sums up his in 'E lucevan' le stelle'. A close look at this famous aria shows both of the descriptive past tenses (the usual and the archaic) working side by side:

1. E **lucevan'**   le stelle...   ed   **olezzava** la terra..
   And were shining the stars,   and was fragrant   the earth...
   —"lucevano" is from **lucere** (to shine, to gleam); "olezzava"
       is from **olezzare**, to be redolent with, etc.

2. e **stridea**   l'uscio   dell'orto...
   and creaked   'the gate'   of the garden...
   —"stridea" is from **stridere**, to creak, etc. An archaic form.

3. e un passo **sfiorava**   la rena...
   and a footstep lightly passed over   the sand...
   —"sfiorava" is from **sfiorare**, to pass lightly over, to skim
                                                          /over

4. **Entrava**   ella,   fragrante,
   She entered,   fragrant,
   —"entrava" is from **entrare**. Note how the past descriptive
       is used   as a simple past tense here.

[4] Both modern and operatic

95

5. ...mi **cadea**   fra   le   braccia,
   she fell (to my advantage!) 'between' (i. e. in) my   arms,
   —"cadea" is from **cadere,** to fall. Note the archaic form.

6. e   mi   **narrava**   di   sè,
   and   to me   she spoke   of herself,
   —"narrava" is from **narrare.**

7. di   me   **chiedea**   con   volubile   impero.
   of me   she asked   with   'chatty' 'authoritativeness'.
   —"chiedea" is the archaic past descriptive of **chiedere,** to ask.

8. Ô   dolci   baci!   languide   carezze!
   Oh, sweet kisses!   languid   caresses!

9. mentr'io fremente   le belle   forme **disciogliea**   dai veli!
   while I, trembling, the beautiful forms released from the veils.

    —"disciogliea" is from **disciogliere,** to undo, to untie. This is
      an interesting, ambivalent line and could refer to Cavaradossi
      the painter releasing perfect artistic forms from chaos (a fa-
      vorite idea of Michelangelo's) and also to Cavaradossi the
      lover helping Tosca to undress. As usual, such subtleties are
      entirely lost in translation.

10. Svanì   per sempre il sogno mio d'amore!
   Vanished   forever   my dream   of love!
   —"svanì" is the simple past of **svanire,** to vanish.

Almost the entire passage is set in the past descriptive, which emphasizes (and even exaggerates?) the continuity and closeness of Mario's love. "Svanì" is the only verb in this aria which is not in the imperfect. It is in the simple past and, having all the directness and forcefulness of that tense, effectively jars Mario (and us too perhaps?) out of the reverie. It would be hard to find a better passage to show a masterful use of contrasting past tenses. One cannot help but think how typical of Puccini it is to create a magic, lyrical bubble of tenderness and hope only to burst it before our very eyes. How important the lyrics are in helping the music to achieve this effect!

96

OTHER PAST TENSES (INDICATIVE MOOD)

Although, as stated earlier, the main purpose of this book is to reduce to **manageable proportions** a large body of knowledge and not clutter your brain with every single grammatical nicety of operatic Italian, there are nevertheless a few other past indicative tenses to mention before tackling the command (or imperative) mood. There are three to look at: the pluperfect, the 'preterite pluperfect', and the conditional past. The most important of these is the pluperfect, which translates the idea of "had". Its forms:

(io) avevo ascoltato	noi avevamo ascoltato
I had listened	we had listened
avevi ascoltato	avevate ascoltato
you had listened	you had listened
aveva ascoltato	avevano ascoltato
she/he had listened	they had listened

Like the compound past, this tense uses either "avere" or "essere" as a helping verb. The difference is that the pluperfect uses a helping verb which is itself in the past descriptive tense. A few examples:

(1) "Sì (Così) grande amor' **dimenticato avea (aveva)(...)**"
Such (a) great love I had forgotten;
(Violetta to Alfredo in **La Traviata**).

(2) "T'avea (aveva) il ciel' per l'amor' creato..."
You had Heaven for love created...
(Heaven had created you for love.) (Radamès to Aïda)

The preterite pluperfect has the same meaning as the pluperfect but uses the preterite of the helping verb. **Congiurare** (to plot) looks like this:

(io) ebbi congiurato	noi avemmo congiurato
I had plotted	we had plotted
avesti congiurato	aveste congiurato
you had plotted	you had plotted
ebbe congiurato	ebbero congiurato
he/she had plotted	they had plotted

The third form, the conditional past, conveys the notion of 'would have done', 'would have been', etc. Its forms:

avrei dato
   I would've given
avresti dato
   you would have...
avrebbe dato
   she would have...

avremmo dato
   we would have given
avreste dato
   you would have given
avrebbero dato
   they would...

As with the other tenses, this tense takes "avere" or "essere" as a helping verb. Some examples:

(1) "Va!   volentieri **obliato** (from **obliare**) l'**avrei**.
Be off with you! Gladly I would have forgotten it
(Otello to Iago)   (the handkerchief)

(2) "E **avrei portato**   la croce crudel'
And I would have carried   the cruel cross

D'angoscie   e   d'onte
Of anguish(es) and   shame(s)

Con   calma   fronte...
With (a) calm   brow...
(Otello to himself)

> *In the original libretto (of **Tosca**) written by Giacosa and Illica, Cavaradossi is made to sing a pompous song of farewell to the world. With a sure instinct, Giacomo realized that a painter with only an hour to live would not waste the hour in formal hymns. The painter is in love. The passage: 'E muoio disperato ... '(...) was written by Giacomo.*
> *(From "Eternal Bohemian", by Dante del Fiorentino). Author's note: Verdi had remarkably similar instincts. See p. 31*

CHAPTER SEVEN

THE IMPERATIVE (COMMAND) MOOD

Referring to Verb Table A (p. 66-7), you will notice that we have dealt with the main tenses of the 'indicative' (or statement) mood: the present, the future, and the past. This leaves only two moods to deal with: the command mood (or 'imperative') and the mood of uncertainty and/or emotion, the subjunctive mood.

The imperative mood is the mood of orders and commands— quite different from making a statement. As such, it is not surprising to find it plays a dominant part in the vocabulary of that seductive bully, Don Giovanni. "Sentimi!" (Listen to me!), "Credimi!" (Believe me!), etc. are typical of him. Again, certain verb tenses and moods do much to set the tone of an opera. There is a political-thematic-psychological dimension to parts of speech i. e. the concept of libretto is inextricably linked to such things as characterization and theme.

The good news about the imperative mood is that it has no future tense and, strictly speaking, no past tense either (although the imperfect subjunctive—See Chapter Nine) does fill that gap.

The imperative can be expressed in all six forms of the conjugation (io, tu, etc.), but three of the six forms are borrowed from the subjunctive. This will be clearer when you look at the forms.

IMPERATIVE OF REGULAR VERBS

1st CONJUGATION (ARE)

ch'io parli! (subjunctive)   parliamo!
    let me speak!   let's speak!
parla! (speak!)   parlate! (speak!)
ch'essa parli! (subjunctive) ch'essi parlino!
    let her speak!   let them speak! (subjunctive)

The 2nd person singular and the 1st and 2nd person plural forms are distinctly and authentically imperative. The other three forms are borrowed from the subjunctive i. e. **they have a subjunctive form but an imperative meaning.** As pure subjunctives they will be dealt with in the next chapter. Note that they are usually preceded by "che" or "ch".

The second conjugation (e. g., **credere**, to believe) looks like this:

ch'io creda! (let me believe!)   crediamo! (let's believe!)
credi! (believe!)   credete! (believe!)
ch'ei creda! (let him believe!) ch'essi credano! (let them
                                                   believe!)

The third conjugation (e. g., **sentire**, to listen, to hear), like this:

ch'io senta! (let me listen!)   sentiamo! (let's listen!)
senti! (listen!)   sentite! (listen!)
ch'essa senta! (let her listen!) ch'esse sentano! (let them
                                                   listen!)

Some typical extracts using the imperative:

(1) "Nessun' **dorma!**" (Let no one sleep!)
    — "dorma" is the 3rd person singular of **dormire**, to sleep.
    (The Principe Ignoto in **Turandot**).

(2) "Ch'io gli **parli!**" (Let me speak to him!)
    — "parli" is the 1st person singular of **parlare**, to speak.
    (Rigoletto to the Courtiers).

(3) "**Senti!** Un bel dì vedremo..." (Listen! One beautiful day we'll see...)
    — "senti" is the 2nd person singular of **sentire**, to listen, etc.
    (Butterfly to Suzuki).

(4) "Lo **ridona** al genitor'!" (Give him i. e. Alfredo back to 'his' father)
    — "ridona" is the 2nd person singular of **ridonare**, to give back.
    (Alfredo's father to Violetta in **La Traviata**).

100

(5) **"Libiamo** nei lieti calici!"
(Let's drink in the happy goblets!)
— "libiamo" is the lst person plural of **libare**,
to drink a toast, etc.
(Violetta to her guests in **La Traviata**).

(6) "Il concetto vi dissi;
The concept you I have told;
Ora **ascoltate** com'egli è svolto!"
Now listen how it is developed!
—"ascoltate" is the 2nd person plural of **ascoltare**,
to listen to.
— (**svolto** comes from **svolgere**).
(Canio to the audience in **I Pagliacci**).

(7) "Ô Dio, **rispondi!**" (Oh, God, reply!)
— "rispondi" is the 2nd person singular of **rispondere**,
to reply.
(Orfeo to Euridice in **Orfeo ed Euridice**).

(8) "**Lasciala,** indegno! **Battiti** meco!"
Leave her, wretch! Fight with me!
— "lascia" is the 2nd person singular of **lasciare**, to leave or
to leave alone; "battiti" is the reflexive
2nd person singular of **battersi**, to fight.
(The Commendatore to Don Giovanni).

(9) "Sol' chi vuole **si serbi** fedele!"
Only whoever wishes, let him keep himself faithful!
— "si serbi" is the (reflexive) 3rd person singular of
serbarsi, to keep oneself, i. e. remain.
(The Duke to Borsa in **Rigoletto**—'Questa o Quella').

(10) "**Osservate, leggete** con me!" (Observe, read with me!)
—"osservate" is the 2nd person plural (used as a singular) of
osservare; "leggete" is the 2nd person plural (used as a
singular) of **leggere**, to read.
(Leporello to Donna Elvira in **Don Giovanni**).

As usual, irregular verbs abound. The following are typical:

ANDARE (to go)   ch'io vada; va; ch'ei vada; andiamo;
                  andate; ch'essi vadano.
AVERE (to have)   ch'io abbia; abbi; ch'ei abbia; abbiamo;
                  abbiate; ch'essi abbiano.
CONOSCERE   ch'io conosca; conosci; ch'ei conosca;
   (to know)   conosciamo; conoscete; ch'essi conoscano.
ESSERE (to be)   ch'io sia; sii; ch'essa sia; siamo; siate;
                  ch'essi siano.
IRE (to go—obsolete) ite (2nd person plural only).
SAPERE (to know) ch'io sappia; sappi; ch'ei sappia; sappiamo;
                  sapete; ch'essi sappiano.
SORGERE (to rise, ch'io sorga; sorgi; ch'essa sorga; sorgiamo;
       get up)   sorgete; ch'ei sorgano.
TACERE   ch'io taccia; taci; ch'ei taccia; tacciamo;
   (to be silent) tacete; ch'essi tacciano.
UDIRE (to hear)   ch'io oda; odi; ch'ei oda; udiamo; udite;
                  ch'essi odano.
VENIRE (to come) ch'io venga; vieni; ch'essa venga;
                  veniamo; venite; ch'essi vengano.

Here they are in context. Note that the third person singular occurs frequently.

(1) "**Sorgi,** mia   dolce speme!"
    Arise,   my   sweet hope!
    — "sorgi" is the 2nd person singular of **sorgere,** to rise.
    ('Lindoro' to Rosina in **Il Barbiere**).
(2) Borsa: "**Tacete!**   C'è   Rigoletto!"
             Be quiet!   It's Rigoletto!
    Ceprano: "Vittoria doppia! L'uccideremo!"
             A double victory! We'll kill him!
    — "tacete" is the 2nd person plural of **tacere,** to be silent.
(3) "**Sii** maladetto!" (Be damned!)
    — "sii" is the 2nd person singular of **essere,** to be.
    (Monterone to Rigoletto).

(4) "Il prigionier' **sia** fucilato!"
The prisoner, let him be shot!
— "sia" is the 3rd person singular of **essere**, to be.
Subjunctive form with an imperative meaning.
(Scarpia to Spoleto in **Tosca**).

(5) "(...) gran dio, **abbi** pietà!"
great god, have pity!
— "abbi" is the 2nd person singular of **avere**, to have.
(Adalgisa to herself in **Norma**).

(6) "Disperso **vada** (che) il mal' pensiero!"
Dispersed let it go (be) the evil thought!
(Let the evil thought be dispersed! i.e. lost)
— "vada" is the 3rd person singular of **andare**, to go.
(Carlo to himself, resisting the temptation to snoop
in Alvaro's personal effects. (**La Forza del Destino**).

(7) "**Ite** sul colle, ô Druidi!"
Go on the hill, oh Druids!
—"ite" is the 2nd person plural of **ire**, to go.
(Oroveso to the Druids in **Norma**).

And here's a short passage with three irregular imperatives. Note the
energy and concision of these imperative/subjunctives.

(8) "Ah, **sappia** alfin' chi l'ama!
Ah, may she know finally who loves her!
— "sappia" is the 3rd person singular of **sapere**, to know,
to realize, etc.
Conosca alfin' chi sono!
May she learn finally who I am!
—"conosca" is the 3rd person singular of **conoscere,**
to know, to discover, etc.
Apprenda ch'anco in trono
May she learn (a) that (c) as well (b) on the throne
—"apprenda" is the 3rd person singular of **apprendere**, to
learn.
Ha degli schiavi Amor'!"
Has (some) slaves Love!
(Love has slaves) (The Duke to the Courtiers in **Rigoletto**).

A peculiarity of the 2nd person singular imperative is that it changes aspect and takes the form of the infinitive when it is used negatively. The examples will clarify this.

(1) "Non **temer'** più nulla, angelo mio!"
Don't fear any longer anything my angel!
— "temer'" is the 2nd person singular of **temere**, to fear.

(2) "Non **sperar'** se non m'uccidi"
Don't hope if you don't kill me

"Ch'io ti lasci fuggir' mai!"
That I you let flee (escape) ever!
— "sperare" is the 2nd person singular of **sperare**, to hope.

(3) "Non **maledir**mi! Non **imprecar**mi!"
Don't curse me! Don't revile me!
(Aïda to Amonasro).

This is really all you need to know about the imperative mood. Before addressing the complexities of the subjunctive, (the last of the three moods—See Table pp. 66-67), test your knowledge with a very contorted passage that would challenge anyone's operatic Italian: the magnificent chorus of the Hebrew slaves in **Nabucco**.

*The chorus from **Nabucco** played an important part in the funeral celebration of Verdi's life. Claudio Sartori writes, "Toscanini conducted 900 voices in the chorus "Val (sic) Pensiero" as the bodies of Verdi and Giuseppina Strepponi were carried from the cemetery to the Rest Center for Musicians (editor's note: it was Verdi himself who financed this rest home). (See photo, p. 31d).*
(Quoted from "The Opera Bedside Book", edited by H. Rosenthal.)

For the chorus, you will find all the vocabulary you need at the end of each verse. (It must be clear by now that the real problem with operatic Italian is not the words themselves but the structure of the phrases, the myriad forms of verbs, etc.) The object of the following exercise is to write a literal translation in the blanks provided then piece it all together in a smooth, free-flowing version (see Chapter Twelve for my version). Note the number of imperatives used in this passage. Also note the inversions and archaic expressions, both typical of operatic Italian.

THE CHORUS FROM **NABUCCO**

1 Va,   pensiero,   sulle   ali   dorate!

___ ___ ___ ___ ___!

VERB NOUN   PREP./ART. NOUN   ADJECTIVE

   il pensiero: the thought;   l'ala: the wing; dorato: golden

2. Va,   ti   posa   sui   clivi,   sui   colli

___ ___ ___ ___ ___ ___

VERB   VERB   PREP./ART.   NOUN   PREP./ART.   NOUN

   posarti: to light on (reflexive); il clivo (slope); il colle (hill)

3. ove   olezzano   tepide   e   molli

___ ___ ___ ___ ___

ADVERB   VERB   ADJECTIVE CONJUNCTION ADJECTIVE

   olezzare: to give off a (pleasant) scent;   molle (soft)

4. l'aure   dolci   del   suolo   natal'.

___ ___ ___ ___ ___

NOUN   ADJECTIVE   PREP./ART   NOUN   ADJECTIVE

   l'aura: the breeze;   il suolo: the earth, soil

5. (3) Del   Giordano   (2) le   rive   (l) saluta

___ ___ ___ ___ ___

PREP./ART.   NOUN   ART.   NOUN   VERB

   il Giordano: the Jordan River;   la riva: the bank (of a river)

6. di　　Sionne　　　le　　torri　　　　atterrate.

PREP.　**NOUN**　　　**ART.**　**NOUN**　　　**ADJECTIVE**
Sionne: Sion;　la torre: the tower;　atterrato: destroyed,
knocked down (past participle used as an adjective).

7. ô,　　mia　patria　sì　　bella　　e　　perduta!
　　　　　　　　　　　　　　　　　　　　　　　　　　　　　　　!
INTERJ.　**ADJ.**　**NOUN**　**ADVERB**　**ADJECTIVE**　**CONJ.**　**ADJECTIVE**
　perduto: lost

8. ô　membranza　　sì　　cara　e　　fatal'!
　　　　　　　　　　　　　　　　　　　　　　　　　　　　　！
INTERJ.　**NOUN**　　**ADVB.**　**ADJECT.**　**CONJ.**　**ADJECTIVE**
　la membranza: the memory, recollection

9. Arpa　d'or'　　dei　　fatidici　　vati,

NOUN　**PREP./NOUN**　**PREP./ART.**　**ADJECTIVE**　**NOUN**
　fatidico: prophetic;　il vate: the poet

10. (l) perchè　(3) muta　(4) (dal　　salice)　(2) pendi?
　　　　　　　　　　　　　　　　　　　　　　　　　　　　?
ADVERB　　**ADJECT.**　　**PREP./ART.**　**NOUN**　　**VERB**
　il salice: the willow tree;　pendere: to hang

11. (2) Le　memorie　(3) nel　　petto　(l) raccendi!
　　　　　　　　　　　　　　　　　　　　　　　　　　　　！
ART.　**NOUN**　　**PREP./ART.**　**NOUN**　**VERB**
　il petto: the breast, chest;　raccendere: to light again

12. Ci　　favella　del　　tempo　che　　fu!
　　　　　　　　　　　　　　　　　　　　　　　　　　！
PRONOUN　**VERB**　**PREP./ART.**　**NOUN**　**PRONOUN**　**VERB**
　favellare: to narrate, tell;　fu: simple past of essere, to be.

106

13. O, (4) simile (6) (di Solima) (5) (ai fati),

———— ———— —— ———— ———— ————,
INTERJ. ADJECT. PREP. NOUN PREP./ART. NOUN
Solima: Jerusalem (Hoare's was the only dictionary which
I could find this in.); il fato: fate, destiny.

14. (1) traggi (2) (un suono) (3) (di crudo lamento)

———— —— ———— ———— ———— ————
VERB ART NOUN PREP. ADJECT. NOUN
traere: to bring; il suono: the sound ("Eh, cumpari!...")

15. o (2) t'ispiri (1) (il Signore) (3) (un concetto)

—— ———— —— ———— —— ————
CONJ. PRON./VERB ART. NOUN ART. NOUN
il concetto: the concept, aphorism, precept.

16. (4) che (6) ne (7) infonda (5) (al patire) (8) virtù!

———— ———— ———— ———— ———— ————!
PRON. PRON. VERB PREP./ ART. VERB (NOUN) NOUN
infondere: to imbue with; patire: to suffer; la virtù:
virtue and/or (martial) courage.

The chorus of the Hebrew slaves, **Nabucco**. Boris Christoff in the
exotic headgear. (The Lyric Opera of Chicago, 1963).

CHAPTER EIGHT

THE PRESENT SUBJUNCTIVE

If you refer back to Verb Table A (p. 66), you will see that of the three moods of the verb, we have dealt with two: the statement (indicative) mood, and the command (imperative) mood.

The only remaining mood is the subjunctive and with it we enter a rather complex and grey area. We have saved the hardest for the last. The subjunctive is the mood of doubt, fear, uncertainty, vagueness and ambiguity. We can say confidently that if you understand the subjunctive you will be able to comprehend the most difficult passages in opera. We can also say that linguistically and thematically you will have penetrated to the innermost core of opera's spirit, which is one of strong emotions (desire, longing, joy, sadness, despair, fear, hatred, thirst for revenge, preoccupation with honor, etc.).

In spite of its complexity, the subjunctive does bring some good news. For one thing, there are no future tenses associated with it. For another, many otherwise irregular verbs follow a predictable pattern in the imperfect subjunctive.

Before examining the forms of the present subjunctive, let us look at how the indicative and the subjunctive typically relate. Pollione's comment to Adalgisa (in **Norma**) will make the point. While attempting to woo this would-be Druid priestess and win her consent to accompany him to Rome, he says to her:

Il	dirò	tanto	che
It	I will say	so much	that (i. e. until)
PRONOUN	**VERB (future—**	**ADVERB**	**CONJUNCTION**
("lo" would	an indicative or		
be more usual	statement mood).		
than "il".)	From **dire**, to say.		

ascoltato	sia	da	te."
(2) listened to	(1) I might be	(3) by	(4) you.
VERB	**HELPING VERB**	**PREPOSITION**	**PRONOUN**
(past participle	(subjunctive of		
of 'ascoltare').	essere, to be).		

The use of two verbs with different moods enables Bellini (and his librettist, Felice Romani) to create nuance: Pollione is determined to keep repeating his message to Adalgisa until she listens to him (hence the future indicative). It is a forceful, straightforward tense. In the second clause an element of doubt or uncertainty is introduced through the use of the subjunctive: maybe Pollione will never succeed in getting Adalgisa to give in to love and follow him to Rome. In this sentence there are two clauses, each with a subject and a verb. The first clause ("Il dirò tanto") has Pollione (understood but not stated) as the subject and "dirò" as a verb. Being able to stand alone, this clause is called the **"principal clause"**. The second clause ("ascoltato sia da te") also has Pollione as the subject, with "ascoltato sia" as the verb (in the present subjunctive). **This second clause makes no sense on its own**, but acquires meaning only if it is connected to the principal clause. This dependency is typical of verb clauses in the subjunctive mood. If this is confusing, don't worry about it: it will soon be clarified by examples.

FORMS OF THE REGULAR PRESENT SUBJUNCTIVE

1st conjugation	2nd conjugation	3rd conjugation
(**pugnare**: to fight)	(**rispondere**: to reply)	(**sentire**: to listen, etc.)

ch'io pugni	ch'io risponda	ch'io senta
(that I might fight, etc.)	(that I might reply, etc.)	(that I might listen, etc.)
che tu pugni	che tu risponda	che tu senta
ch'ei pugni	ch'ei risponda	ch'ei senta
che pugniamo	che rispondiamo	che sentiamo
che pugniate	che rispondiate	che sentiate
che pugnino	che rispondano	che sentano

Examples of regular verbs in the present subjunctive:

1. "Ch'io ti **punisca** è scritto / Sul libro del destin'."
   That I you should punish is written / 'in' the book of destiny.
   — "punisca" is the present subjunctive of **punire**, to punish.
   Why a subjunctive is required here will soon be explained.
   (Carlo to Alvaro in **La Forza del Destino**).

2. "E la fuggevol' ora,
   And the fleeting hour,

   s'innebrii a voluttà!"
   let it 'intoxicate itself' 'as it wishes' i. e. to the point of
   voluptuousness.

   — "s'innebrii": present subjunctive of **innebriarsi**, to 'intoxicate onself'. This is the subjunctive which does double duty
   as an imperative. (See Chapter Seven.) It is clear from passages such as this that if you translate them accurately, you
   are forced to use clumsy, unidiomatic English. Again, the
   only solution to this problem is to master the original.
   (Alfredo to Violetta in **La Traviata**).

As usual, the irregular verbs will be unpredictable. Some examples:

AVERE (TO HAVE)
   ch'io abbia che noi abbiamo (that we might have)
   che tu abbia che voi abbiate
   ch'essa abbia ch'essi abbiano
      (that she might have)

ESSERE (TO BE)
   ch'io sia (or **fia***: obsolete) che siamo
   che tu sia che siate
   ch'ei sia (that he might be) che siano

---

* **Note** that the "fia" here is easily confused with the "fia"
of the irregular future (see pp. 75,76).

110

FARE (TO MAKE, DO, COMMIT, ETC.)

ch'io	faccia	che	facciamo
che tu	faccia	che (voi)	facciate
ch'essa	faccia	ch'esse	facciano

(that she might commit, etc.)

SAPERE (TO KNOW, TO FIND OUT, ETC.—usually
implies factual or certain knowledge)

ch'io	sappia	che sappiamo
che tu	sappia	che sappiate
ch'egli	sappia	che sappiano

(that he might know, find out)

TACERE (TO BE SILENT, TO 'SHUT UP')

ch'io	taccia	che	tacciamo
che tu	taccia	che	tacciate
ch'essa	taccia	che'essi	tacciano (that they might

(that she might   be silent)
be silent)

VEDERE (TO SEE)

ch'io	veda (or vegga)	che	vediamo/veggiamo
che tu	veda (or vegga)	che	vediate/veggiate
ch'egli	veda (or vegga)	ch'essi	vedano/veggano

(that he might see)   (that they might see)

An example:

1. "Bisogna   che tutti **abbiano** per morto il Cavalier'!"
It is necessary that everyone 'consider' as dead the 'Cavalier'!
— "abbiano" is the 3rd person plural of **avere**, to have. The
subjunctive is always used when you have "bisogna che"
in the principle clause.
(Scarpia to Spoleto in **Tosca**).

As stated earlier, the subjunctive is a complex, subtle mood. In order to understand it better, it helps to break it down into four types. The subjunctive is used: (1) as an imperative (See the last chapter.); (2) after another verb which is in the imperative; (3) after a verb (in another clause) which conveys emotion (fear, uncertainty, etc.); (4) after certain expressions (e. g., the "bisogna che" contained in the example above).

1. THE SUBJUNCTIVE AS AN IMPERATIVE

This kind of subjunctive has already been dealt with (p. 99 ff.). When Rigoletto insists on speaking to the Duke, he says, "Ch'io gli **parli!**" (Let me speak to him!) This is the subjunctive used as a command (imperative).

2. THE SUBJUNCTIVE AFTER A VERB IN THE IMPERATIVE

(a) "Fa   ch'io **rida,**   Buff<u>o</u>n'!"
    Make   that I laugh,   Jester!
    — "fa": imperative of **fare,** to make, etc.
    — "rida": subjunctive of **r<u>i</u>dere,** to laugh.
    (The Duke to Rigoletto)

(b) "Ch'io   vi   **lasci,**   assentite!"
    That I   you   leave,   grant!
    — "assentite": imperative of **assentire,** to consent, grant.
      2nd person plural used as a singular.
    —"lasci": subjunctive of **lasciare,** to leave.
      1st person singular.

(c) "Non sper<u>a</u>r', se non m'uccidi,   ch'io ti **lasci** fugg<u>i</u>r' mai!"
    Don't hope, if you don't kill me, that I you let flee   ever!
                              (...) that I ever let you flee!
    — "Non sper<u>a</u>r'": imperative of **sperare,** to hope. 2nd person
      singular. (Note the infinitive form with the negative.)
    — "lasci": subjunctive of **lasciare,** to leave, abandon, etc.
      1st person singular. (Donna Anna to Don Giovanni).

112

3. THE PRESENT SUBJUNCTIVE USED AFTER VERBS OF EMOTION (DOUBT, VAGUENESS, UNCERTAINTY, BELIEF, PERCEPTION, FEAR, DESIRE, WILL, ETC.)

(a) "Ma mi   par'   che **venga**   gente!"
But to me it seems that (are coming) people!
   — "par'": present indicative (statement mood) of **parere**, to seem, to appear. 3rd person singular.
   — "venga": present subjunctive of **venire**, to come. 3rd person singular. "Venga" implies uncertainty: maybe someone is coming and then again, maybe not. (Leporello in **Don Giovanni**).

(b) "Non si   picca se **sia**   ricca,
He doesn't take pride if she might be rich,

se **sia**   brutta, se **sia**   bella..."
if she might be ugly, if she might   be beautiful..."
   — "si picca": present indicative of **piccarsi**, to take pride in, to worry about, etc. 3rd person singular.

   —"sia": present subjunctive of **essere**, to be. 3rd person singular. "Sia" is deliberately vague. Don Giovanni's taste in women is very accommodating. Pretty, ugly, fat, thin, short, tall -- it's all the same.

4. THE PRESENT SUBJUNCTIVE AFTER CERTAIN EXPRESSIONS (TIME, OBLIGATION, ETC.).

Here are some of the expressions which are always followed by a verb in the subjunctive mood:

   — **benchè:**   although
   — **bisogna che:**   it is necessary that
   — **è d'uopo che:**   it is necessary that
   — **fino a che:**   until
   — **è mestiere che:** it is necessary that
   — **prima che:**   before

Some examples:

(a) "Egli è mestiere/ che tu subito **cada**..."
    It is necessary/ that you immediately fall...
    —"cada": present subjunctive of **cadere**, to fall.
    2nd person singular. A subjunctive is required after "**è mestiere che**". (Tosca to Cavaradossi).
    Note the pleonastic (merely a gap-filler) "egli".

(b) "M'arde ogni fibra! Ch'io ti **vegga** è d'uopo!"
    Burns (in) me every fibre! (That I) you see (It) is necessary.
    (I must see you! Every fibre burns in me!)
    — "vegga": present subjunctive of **vedere**, to see. 1st person singular. A subjunctive is needed after "**è d'uopo che**".
    (The Count in **Il Trovatore**)

(c) "Verrò a gridare fino a che **vegga**
    I will come to shout until/as long as I see

    restarsi inulto di mia famiglia l'atroce insulto!"
    remain unavenged of my family the atrocious insult!
    (the atrocious insult of my family remain unavenged)
    — "vegga": present subjunctive of **vedere**, to see.
    1st person singular. "**Fino a che**" must be followed by the subjunctive.
    (Rigoletto in **Rigoletto**)

5. OTHER USES OF THE PRESENT SUBJUNCTIVE

Some uses of the subjunctive don't neatly fit any of the above categories.

(a) The subjunctive is used after a superlative or a categorical statement.
    "Non v'è più alcuno / che qui **rispondami?**"
    Is there no longer anyone / who here might reply to me?
    —"risponda": present subjunctive of **rispondere**, to reply.
    3rd person singular. "Alcuno" is operatic for the modern "nessuno". (Gilda to herself in **Rigoletto**.)

114

The following two passages show how complex the subjunctive can be:

(a) "Non **sia** mai che   **s'offuschi**   il suo cand<u>o</u>r'!"
Let it never be that (should be darkened) her whiteness
                                                     (purity)!
— "s<u>i</u>a": present subjunctive of **essere**, to be.
   3rd person singular.
— "s'offuschi": present subjunctive of **offuscarsi**,
   to 'darken oneself', to become dark.

The subjunctive in the first clause ("s<u>i</u>a") is the imperative type explained on pp. 99, 100. The verb in the second clause, **offuscarsi**, must go in the subjunctive as well because it follows an imperative. It this seems rather complicated, it is, but that's the way librettos often are. It could be argued, however, that it is only fitting that the diabolical complexity of Rigoletto's mind should be conveyed in twisted syntax and that this is one of the ways in which Verdi (and Piave, and Victor Hugo) have managed to create an extremely interesting character. As usual, the more you understand of the original Italian, the deeper and more accurate your grasp of the opera.

Otello's eloquent phrases in the great love scene with Desd<u>e</u>-mona use the power of the imperative/subjunctive to advantage:

(b) "**Venga** la morte! mi **colga**   nell'<u>e</u>stasi
Let death come!   Let seize me   in the ecstasy

Di quest'amplesso   il momento supremo!"
Of this embrace   the supreme moment!
(Let the (...) moment seize me in the ecstasy of this embrace.)

— "venga": present subjunctive (imperative) of **venire**,
   to come. 3rd person singular.
— "colga": present subjunctive (imperative) of **c<u>o</u>gliere**,
   to seize. 3rd person singular.

The syntax here is unusual and highly effective. The subject, "il momento supremo", is revealed only at the end of the sentence (which is technically known as a 'periodic sentence'). This creates the effect of a short but intense dramatic crescendo. On one level the passage seems to mean "Let the supreme moment seize me in the ecstasy of this embrace!" On another level one senses a sexual innuendo in that "momento supremo". (A little hint of it, anyway.) This is the kind of insight you acquire with knowledge of the original libretto. Note also the characteristic Latinism, "amplesso" (embrace); the modern Italian would be "abbraccio" or "abbracciata".

Can you identify some of the subjunctive forms and nail down the various reasons why each of the following extracts is written in the present subjunctive? (5 possible reasons)

(1) "Fate ch'io   sappia (from sapere, to know) la madre mia!"
'Do such things'   so that I might know   my mother!
(Untranslatable i. e. Tell me about my mother, cause me to know her, etc.)   (Gilda to Rigoletto.)

REASON FOR THE SUBJUCTIVE: _____.

(2) "Io vo' che   sia magnifica   la festa, e (i) canti (...)"
I want (that)   to be magnificent   the party, and songs (...)
I want the party to be magnificient (...)
(The Count to the wedding guests in Le Nozze di Figaro.)

REASON FOR THE SUBJUNCTIVE: _____
WHAT INFINITIVE IS 'SIA' FROM?   _____

(3) "(...) m'ascolta!"
Listen to me!
Bench'io finga (from fingere, pretend) d'amarlo, odio quel
Although I pretend to love him, I hate that Moor!   /Moro!"
(Iago to Roderigo in Otello).

REASON FOR THE SUBJUNCTIVE: _____

116

(4) "Il sacro brando   dal Dio temprato,   Per tua   man'
The sacred sword by the God tempered, Through your hand

Diventi (from **diventare**) ai nemici terror', fulgore, morte!"
Let it become   to the enemies terror, lightning, death!
(Ramfis, the High Priest, to Radamès in **Aïda**).

REASON FOR THE SUBJUNCTIVE: _____

(5) "Ah, pria che **giunga** all'altar',   **si rapisca!** (from **rapire**)"
Ah, before she arrives at the altar, 'let her be abducted'!
The reflexive "si" in "**si rapisca**" is similar to the one used
by the Prologue in **I Pagliacci** when he asks permission to
come on stage: "Si può?!" (May I?) i. e. "si" here can refer
to almost anyone as the subject of the action. In English we
have to translate into the **passive** ('Let her be abducted!')
but notice the concision and power of the **active voice** used
in the Italian.
(The Count to Ferrando, referring to Leonora, **Trovatore**.)

REASON FOR 'GIUNGA' BEING IN THE
SUBJUNCTIVE: _____

(6) "Qual'   tu   **sia**,   donde   **venga**,
Which(ever) you might be,   where(ever) you come (from),

Io   già   saper'   non voglio!"
I   certainly   to know don't want!
I certainly don't want to know!
(Silva to Ernani).

REASON FOR 'SIA' AND 'VENGA' BEING IN THE
SUBJUNCTIVE: _____

WHICH INFINITIVE IS 'VENGA' FROM? _____
(Answers in Chapter 12).

CHAPTER NINE

THE IMPERFECT SUBJUNCTIVE

The present subjunctive and the imperfect subjunctive are related to each other in much the same way as the present indicative and the descriptive past. (See page 66). One of the curiosities of operatic Italian is the extent to which the subjunctive is used. The present subjunctive is used a **great deal**; the imperfect subjunctive has a smaller part to play, but it occurs more often than one would expect. Doubtless this can be explained in part by the tendency of librettists and composers to seek out, rather than to avoid, difficult forms. The imperfect subjunctive is the most difficult of the verb tenses so if you understand it, your ability to fathom librettos will be greatly enhanced.

In the three regular conjugations, the imperfect subjunctive looks like this:

1st **PUGNARE**	2nd **TEMERE**	3rd **FINIRE**
(to fight)	(to fear)	(to finish)
ch'io pugnassi	ch'io temessi	ch'io finissi
che tu pugnassi	che tu temessi	che tu finissi
ch'ei pugnasse	ch'ei temesse	ch'ei finisse
che pugnassimo	che (noi) temessimo	che finissimo
che (voi) pugnaste	che temeste	che finiste
ch'essi pugnassero	che temessero	che finissero

Some examples of its use:

(1) "Se il Duca vostro d'appressarsi **osasse,**
If your Duke to approach should dare,

Ch'ei non entri, gli dite..."
Let him not enter, to him say..."

118

— "osasse": imperfect subjunctive (3rd person singular)
  of **osare,** to dare. Note that Italian uses a **past tense**
  (the imperfect subjunctive) in order to convey a **future**
  possibility. Note as well the present subjunctive ("entri")
  used an an imperative.
  (Rigoletto to the Courtiers).

(2) "Nei brevi   istanti,   **prima che**   il mio presagio interno
In the brief moments, before   my   'premonition'

Sull'orma   corsa   ancora mi **spingesse.**"
On the track already run (i. e. followed) yet me had pushed.
(Had yet pushed me onto the path already run.)

— "spingesse": imperfect subjunctive (3rd person singular) of
  spingere, to push. As we have seen, the subjunctive mood
  is always used after 'prima che'. "Corsa" is the irregular
  past participle of **correre,** to run. Notice the contorted
  structure of the second verse. As stated earlier, operatic
  Italian is nothing if not complex and in passages like the
  one above such complexity demands much of both the
  performers and the audience. Terseness adds to the difficulty. These two verses are particularly important because
  they explain how the Duke almost accidentally discovers
  that Gilda is his own jester's daughter.

Many otherwise irregular verbs have regular imperfect subjunctives,
but some imperfect subjunctives might surprise you:

DARE (to give)
   ch'io dessi   che noi dessimo
   che tu dessi   che deste
   ch'essa desse   ch'essi dessero
ESSERE (to be)
   ch'io fossi   che fossimo
   che (tu) fossi   che foste
   ch'ei fosse   ch'essi fossero

FARE (to make, do, commit, etc.)

ch'io	facessi	che (noi)	facessimo
che (tu)	facessi	che (voi)	faceste
ch'essa	facesse	ch'essi	facessero

Some examples of the irregular imperfect subjunctive in action:

(1) "Se   il   serto   regal' a   me   **desse**   il   poter'
If (only) the regal crown to   me   gave   the power

di leggere   nei   cor'...   che   Dio   sol'   può veder'!"
to read   in the hearts... which God   alone can see!

— "desse": imperfect subjunctive (3rd person singular) of
dare, to give. "If only God gave me" or "If only God
would give me" or "I wish that God would give me!":
this kind of wishful thinking is typical of the imperfect
subjunctive. We could call the imperfect subjunctive the
Don Quixote of the verb tenses for its tendency to create a
climate of non-resolution, vagueness, unrealistic wishes
and impossible dreams. (King Philip in **Don Carlo**).

(2) "Se   quel guerrier'   io   **fossi**!
If only that warrior   I   were!

Se il mio sogno   **s'avverasse**!"
If my dream   only were to come true!

(Radamès in 'Celeste Aïda')
— "fossi": imperfect subjunctive (1st person singular) of
essere to be.
— "s'avverasse": imperfect subjunctive of **avverarsi**, to
come true, 'to realize itself'. Such are the dreams of the
young hero. We might say that Radamès' subjunctive
won't change to an indicative until he becomes certain of
his new identity as the chosen leader.

Concerning the details of usage, the imperfect subjunctive sometimes parallels the present subjunctive and sometimes is used in
ways which are peculiar to it alone. The first three categories below
(A to C) have counterparts in the present subjunctive (pp. 112-14).

A. THE IMPERFECT SUBJUNCTIVE AS AN IMPERATIVE.

(1) When the Conte di Luna speaks of tracking Azucena down
and killing her, his wish is expressed as an imperfect subjunctive:

"O, dato mi **fosse** rintracciarla un dì!"
Ah, given to me (if only it were) to hunt her down one day!
(Ah, if only it were given to me to hunt her down one day!)
— "fosse": imperfect subjunctive (3rd person singular) of
essere, to be. Note that "fosse dato" is also in the passive
voice i. e. the Conte di Luna, who is the subject, also
stands to receive the action (which accounts for the indirect object pronoun "mi", outlined on p. 53).
(Ferrando to the Count's soldiers, etc., **Il Trovatore**).

(2) Amneris' longing for Radamès goes well in the imperfect
subjunctive:
"O, s'ei **potesse** amarmi!"
Ah, if only he could love me!
— "potesse": imperfect subjunctive
(3rd person singular) of **potere**, to be able to.

(3) "Ah, cogliere **potessi** il traditore che sì mi sturba!"
Ah, seize (if only I could) the traitor who thus me disturbs!
— "potessi": imperfect subjunctive (lst person singular) of
potere. When used as a wish or imperative, the imperfect
subjunctive sometimes is preceded by "se" (if) and sometimes is not. (The Duke in soliloquy in **Rigoletto**).

121

B. THE IMPERFECT SUBJUNCTIVE AFTER VERBS OF EMOTION

(DOUBT, UNCERTAINTY, VAGUENESS, FEAR, WISHING, DESIRING, ETC.)

These are similar to the ones already discussed on p. 113. Typically, the **principal clause** has a verb in the indicative; **the dependent** clause has a verb in the subjunctive. Some examples should clarify this:

(1) "Son' felice che nulla a voi **nuocesse** l'aria di questa notte."
I am happy that in no way   harmed you the air of this night.
— "nuocesse": imperfect subjunctive (3rd person singular) of **nocere**, to harm. (Rigoletto to the Courtiers).

(2) The next example says a great deal in a few words. Again we find operatic Italian capable in incredible concision:

"Che di Ceprano noi la Contessa/Rapir' **volessimo**, stolto,
/credè!"
That of Ceprano we the Countess/To abduct wished, foolish,
/he believed!

— "volessimo": imperfect subjunctive of **volere**, to wish, to want. Rearranged in its normal word order, the above passage would look like this:

INDICATIVE CLAUSE:

"Stolto,   credè   che noi   **volessimo**
Foolish man, he (Rigoletto) thought that we (courtiers) wanted

SUBJUNCTIVE CLAUSE:

rapir'   la Contessa di Ceprano.
to abduct   the Countess of Ceprano. (as opposed to Gilda, whom they themselves wrongly believe to be Rigoletto's mistress.)

Once unravelled, the Courtiers' statement clearly fits the classic indicative clause-with-subjunctive clause pattern. The first clause has Rigoletto as the (understood) subject with a verb of opinion in the indicative ("credè"). This principal clause is then connected to a dependent clause in the subjunctive ("noi" is the subject, and "volessimo rapir'" is the complete verb). Both verbs are in past tenses.

The two verses analyzed above provide an extreme example of two common characteristics of operatic Italian: twisted word order (see p. 7) and concision. Concision is necessitated by the contractive metamorphosis which any written words (e. g., in a tragedy) must undergo in their passage to sung words (opera). Brevity might be the soul of wit, but one must admit that some operatic passages do go to the extreme. Mr. Henry Simon has some good observations on this transformation process:

> The principal problems in adapting (...) **Macbeth** for the operatic stage were the same ones a librettist always finds in adapting a spoken play for lyric purposes—the problems of condensation and of simplification. Condensation -- drastic condensation -- is necessary for a very simple reason: it takes less time to utter any sentiment in spoken words than it does when the same words are set to music. Even a short, dramatic line like "Is this a dagger which I see before me?", unaccompanied as it is in Verdi's score, must be measured out in the dotted eighths, sixteenths, and quarter notes of a recitative style, and the whole speech punctuated with dramatic chords in the orchestra (...). **Macbeth** is one of Shakespeare's shorter plays, but the libretto, though its playing time is at least as long, has room for barely half the number of words. Some scenes, some actions, had to be sacrificed." (Quoted from the introduction to the RCA Victor recording of **Macbeth**).

The imperfect subjunctive really is an important key to understanding operatic Italian, so here are a few more examples of this
tense/mood used with verbs of emotion:

(1) "Bramò   che   il   signor' nostro
    He desired that our   master

    a lui   **giurasse**   di non cessar' le   indagini."
    to him should swear   not to stop   the investigation(s).

— "giurasse": imperfect subjunctive (3rd person singular) of
  giurare, to swear to something, to take an oath. The
  principal clause has "bramò" (preterite or simple past) as
  its verb; the subordinate clause has "giurasse".) Note the
  word "indagini",which illustrates two now-familiar difficulties: stress and idiom. There is surely no way of guess-
  ing that "indagini" is accented on the second syllable. Nor
  is it possible to explain why Italian prefers the plural ("investigations") and English favors the singular. All we can
  say is that the two beasts have different natures.
  (The extract is from **Il Trovatore**).

(2) "A   te   chiedeva,   ô   Dio,
    To   thee   I asked,   oh   God,
    Ch'ella   **potesse**   ascendere
    That she (Gilda) might be able   to ascend
    Quanto   caduto   er'io."
    As much as   I had   fallen.
— "potesse": imperfect subjunctive (3rd person singular) of
  potere, to be able to. The principal clause contains the
  verb "chiedeva" (in opera the 1st person singular imperfect
  indicative sometimes borrows the 3rd person singular
  form); the subordinate clause contains "potesse".

C. THE IMPERFECT SUBJUNCTIVE USED
AFTER CERTAIN EXPRESSIONS
(BENCHÈ; BISOGNA CHE; È D'UOPO CHE; FINO A CHE; PRIMA CHE; ETC.)

These closely parallel those mentioned earlier in connection with the present subjunctive (pp. 113-14).

(1) "Ella   mi   fu   rapita!
She ('to my detriment') was   abducted!

E   quando,   ô   ciel?
And when,   oh   Heaven?

Ne'   brevi   istanti
In the   brief   moments

prima che   il mio   presagio   interno
before   my   'internal   premonition'

sull'orma   corsa   ancora   mi   **spingesse!**"
on the path   (already) taken   yet   had pushed me!
(See p. 119 for further remarks on the same passage).

D. OTHER USES OF THE IMPERFECT
SUBJUNCTIVE.

Sometimes the imperfect subjunctive is used in ways which have no parallel in the present subjunctive. The most common example is when the verb follows "se" (which usually means "**if**" but can also mean "**if only**").

(1) "Se quel   guerrier'   io **fossi!**
If only   that warrior   I   were!   (If only I were ...!)
(Radamès in 'Celeste Aïda')
— "fossi": imperfect subjunctive (1st person singular) of **essere**. Here 'se' conveys the idea of a wish: 'If only I were!...' When the imperfect subjunctive is used in this way it carries the idea of an imperative (a wish for the self).

125

(2) "Ô   Re,   se   non   **foss'io**   grand'Inquisitor'!..."
Oh   King, if only I weren't   (the) Grand Inquisitor!
(The Grand Inquisitor to Philip in **Don Carlo**).
— "foss'" (**fossi**) here simply means "were".
This construction seems peculiar to Italian.

This completes the verb chart. How much of it can you remember? To find out, here is the first part of the famous sextet from **Lucia**. Can you find all of the **22** verbs? Can you name the tense of each? As usual, see Chapter 12 for the answers.

Edgardo: 1.   Chi mi frena in tal' momento?
         2.   Chi troncò dell'ira il corso?
         3.   Il suo duolo, il suo spavento
         4.   Son(o) la prova d'un rimorso!
         5.   Ma, qual' rosa inaridita
         6.   Ella sta tra morte e vita.
         7.   Io son(o) vinto, son(o) commosso!
         8.   T'amo, ingrata, t'amo ancor'!

Enrico: 9.   Chi mi frena il mio furore
        10.   E la man' che al brando corse?
        11.   Della misera in favore
        12.   Nel mio petto un grido sorse!
        13.   È (è) mio sangue! L'ho tradita!
        14.   Ella sta tra morte e vita...
        15.   Ah, chè spegnere non posso
        16.   I rimorsi del mio cor'!?

Lucia: 17.   Io sperai che a me la vita
        18.   Tronca(to) avesse il mio spavento!
        19.   Ma la morte non m'aita (aiuta)!
        20.   Vivo ancor' per il mio tormento!
        21.   Da miei lumi cadde il velo!
        22.   Mi tradì la terra e il cielo!
        23.   Vorrei pianger', ma non posso
        24.   M'abbandona il pianto ancor'!

126

Before tying up the loose ends (Chapter Ten: Idioms), observe the following diagram which summarizes much of what you have learned so far about operatic Italian. The aria is from **Lucia**. Enrico Ashton is determined to increase his family's power by marrying off his sister, Lucia, to a strong ally, Arturo Bucklaw. Enrico realizes that his plans are endangered when Normanno, his chief huntsman, informs him that Lucia has been seen regularly at dawn in the company of Edgardo, the Ravenswoods' enemy. Enrico vents his anger and frustration in the powerful 'Cruda, funesta smania':

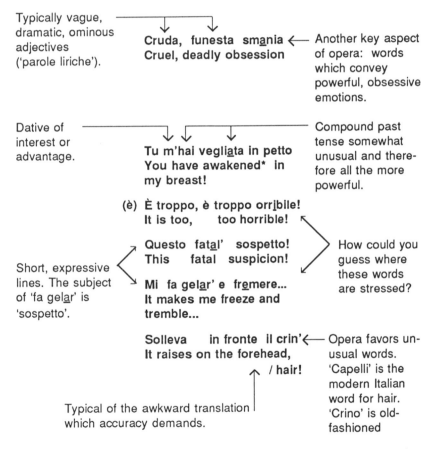

Typically vague, dramatic, ominous adjectives ('parole liriche').

Cruda, funesta smania ← Another key aspect
Cruel, deadly obsession of opera: words which convey powerful, obsessive emotions.

Dative of interest or advantage.

Tu m'hai vegliata in petto
You have awakened* in my breast!

Compound past tense somewhat unusual and therefore all the more powerful.

(è) **È troppo, è troppo orribile!**
It is too, too horrible!

Short, expressive lines. The subject of 'fa gelar' is 'sospetto'.

Questo fatal' sospetto!
This fatal suspicion!

Mi fa gelar' e fremere...
It makes me freeze and tremble...

How could you guess where these words are stressed?

Solleva in fronte il crin' ← Opera favors unusual words.
It raises on the forehead,
/ hair! 'Capelli' is the modern Italian word for hair. 'Crino' is old-fashioned

Typical of the awkward translation which accuracy demands.

No doubt by now you are able to recognize what makes operatic Italian special. Now for the final area, and a grey one it is: idioms.

* (to my disadvantage)

CHAPTER TEN

WHAT GRAMMAR CAN'T EXPLAIN: IDIOMS.

Chances are that you are now able to decipher 95 percent of most librettos. All you need is a good dictionary, an irregular verb table and perhaps an excellent bilingual version such as William Weaver's "Verdi Librettos". The remaining five percent of what you have to learn consists of usage which does not easily fit any of the patterns examined in the first nine chapters of this book. This usage generally falls into two categories: idioms and special verb tenses.

Idioms are the unpredictable ways of expressing things peculiar to a language. English has thousands of them. The French wisely call them "idiotismes" and it is true that there is no particular logic to them: you just have to be on the lookout. If you encounter a phrase which doesn't make sense, then it is probably an idiom and you must look up its meaning in the dictionary. Sooner or later you get used to them and they don't pose much of a problem. The following is only a sampling of what you'll find in librettos:

IDIOMS

(1) "Speme non v'ha per egli!" (There is no hope for him.)
"ha" comes from **avere** (to have), but this has nothing to do with logic.

(2) "Vincerà la stessa morte." (He will overcomes death itself.)
"Stessa" usually means "the same". This doesn't help much.

(3) "Non me la sento." (I don't feel like it.) From **sentirsela** , but this information doesn't account for its meaning.

(4) "Quali cure!" (How kind! How attentive!)

(5) "Sarà!" (That's probably so! You're doubtless right!)
Figaro (**Il Barbiere**)

(6) "Peggio per voi!" (Too bad for you! That's your hard luck! etc.) (Sparafucile to Rigoletto).

(7) "Avrò dunque sognato!" (Therefore I must have dreamt it.)
Rigoletto to Marullo. A future past tense with a special meaning.

128

(8) "Usc<u>i</u>tene!" (Leave! Get out of here!) The "ne" has no meaning and doubtless is used here to accommodate the phrasing of the music. 'Pleonastic' is the technical term for this kind of superfluous word (see page 8); we saw it earlier in connection with "pure" (p. 46)
(Gilda to "Gualtier Maldè" in **Rigoletto**.)

(9) "Ti veggo a me d'accanto." (I see you beside me.)
(Leonora to Manrico in **Il Trovatore**.)

(10) "(...) questa lama/ Vibra, immergi all'<u>e</u>mpio in cor'" (...this blade/'Stick', plunge into that wretch's heart!) Referring back to the dative of advantage (see pp. 53-4), the idiom makes sense: "immergi in cor' all'<u>e</u>mpio" ('immerse in the heart to the disadvantage of the wretch'). As I mentioned earlier, in order to be faithful to the original Italian, the English translation can't help but be clumsy yet **it is only by doing this kind of clumsy literal translation exercise that you learn to appreciate what the words really mean.** Again, opera doesn't yield its deepest meaning easily.

(11) "Guai se l'arcano affetto/A noi leggesse in core!" (Woe unto us if she should read the hidden affection which we have in our heart.) Again, the dative of advantage part of the idiom ('a noi') is almost impossible to translate. This example is similar to the one in item ten above. Such constructions are very common in opera (Radam<u>è</u>s to Aïda).

VERBS

As might be expected, verbs pose a number of peculiarities. The passive 'voice' is a common one. "Fu presa." means "She was taken prisoner." (Ferrando speaking of Azucena's mother in **Il Trovatore**.) In a passive voice the subject receives the action:

(1) "Lui fu tradito da me." (He was betrayed by me,) The subject here is "lui" (egli). The person doing the betraying is "me".

(2) "Da un g<u>e</u>nio d'inferno qui fosti guidato!" (By a demon from hell you were led here.) (The Courtiers to Monterone in **Rigoletto**.) "Fosti" is the irregular simple past of **essere**.

129

(3) "Fu presa e al rogo fu condannata." (She was seized and to the stake condemned.) (Ferrando in **Il Trovatore**.)

Another peculiarity is the verb (in the infinitive) used as a noun:

(1) "col favellar' del cor'" (**favellare**, to speak, discourse on)
With the 'confiding' of the heart.

There are also some special kinds of present tenses:

(1) "Sto reggendo." (I am holding firm i.e. bearing up.)
The present tense of **stare** is used as the helping verb.

(2) "Va scorrendo, va scorrendo..." (It i. e. malicious gossip keeps on running down i.e. rushing along) The present tense of "andare" used as a helping verb gives the phrase this shade of meaning. (Don Basilio to Don Bartolo in **Il Barbiere**.)

And there are some uses of the reflexive (see pp. 55; 71,72) which I thought best to explain now. Reflexives are often used to generalize about people: "Non s'ebbe contezza mai."* (No one ever heard anything.) "Ebbe" is the simple past of **avere** (to have). The translation conveys the idea of the original but doesn't account for its construction; you have to recognize the reflexive and know this particular use of it. Reflexives can also convey the notion of the English "one" (or the French "on"): "Com'usasi pagar'?" (How does one usually pay?) as Rigoletto asks that scrupulous business-man-assassin, Sparafucile.

* "contezza" literally means precise information.

CHAPTER ELEVEN

THE LIBRETTO IN PERSPECTIVE

By now you have enough Italian to cope with most librettos. How good are they? Are there any really good ones or was Piave right to dismiss himself as a mere 'poetaster'? How do you tell a good libretto from a bad one? What criteria should be brought to bear? This is a complex issue and would require another book to do it justice. Nevertheless, before closing I would like to leave you with a few ideas on evaluation criteria.

Taking the overview, the quality of a libretto very much depends on the quality of other things: plot, characterization, depth and interest of themes, and atmosphere. Obviously it makes for a good libretto if it is based on the work of giants like Shakespeare and Schiller. (Iago's 'Credo in un Dio Crudel'' is the best kind of writing because it develops character, theme and atmosphere in a few lines.) From the narrower perspective of the libretto's rhetorical capabilities, we have already seen the importance of such things as sonority (p. 3), literary associations (p. 2) and richness of connotation, including puns (pp. 3, 5, 39, 51). There are other criteria as well, but I will limit my discussion to: (1) evocative power; (2) proliferation; (3) poetic devices and originality of language; (4) wit.

Perhaps the most important of these is **evocative power**. This is what Verdi looked for above all else in his librettos. The quest for **just the right word** (accurate, mood-setting, evocative, orginal) must have driven him and his librettists to exhaustion. Verdi summed it up well in his remarks to Ghislanzoni (already quoted on page 33) when he refered to those magical, evocative phrases which seem predestined to be married to his music. "Parole liriche" describes them well. Many such phrases have already been quoted in this book ("Ed olezzava la terra"—p. 94; "Qual' piuma al vento"—p. 19; "stanco di gloria e onor'"—p.23; "Libiamo ne' lieti calici!"—p. 25). These words are the mood-setters which I mentioned earlier (p. 33).

Let's look closely at a few other examples and see why they are effective. **Aïda**. Amneris is smitten with Radamès and says to him:

"Di quale nobil' **fierezza** ti **balena** il volto!"
With what noble   pride your face 'becomingly' (ti) lights up!

"Fierezza" is an excellent word, not just for the sound (somewhat harsh and savage) but for its connotations (wild, pagan, arrogant, even cruel) which are appropriate to the pre-Christian world of the Pharaohs. ("Superbo" is a close synonym, but its Christian rather than pagan connotations make it less suitable.) "Balena" is also very suggestive. It comes from "balenare", usually used to describe lightning's sudden burst of light. Highly appropriate here, it suggests sudden desert storms, and flashes of true emotion glimpsed in the eyes of courtly sophisticates who, like Amneris, have become experts in the art of dissimulation.

Another parola lirica. This time from **Cavalleria Rusticana**. Turiddu is saying farewell (addio) to his mother just in case he doesn't return from the duel with Alfio:

Troppi	bicchier'	ne	ho	tracannati!
Too many	glasses	of it	I have	gulped down!
Vado	fuori	all'aperto.		
I am going	outside	in the open.		

"Vado fuori all'aperto." The phrase is so simple, natural, and euphonious yet it has menacing undertones which become clear only after several listenings. Such is all poetry. Note the Sophoclean irony: Mamma Lucia is meant to understand only that her son needs a breath of air; we realize that Turiddu is about to meet a cruel fate. The power of the parola lirica here is reinforced by the music itself (there's something piquant and sinister in that B minor phrase) and the innocent everyday word "fuori" (outside) is an ironic connective because it's the last thing that Alfio himself says to Turiddu before leaving him: "io v'aspetto (I await you) qui fuori." How apt that two heroic rustics use the same words!

132

When the right words come in a cluster a special power is achieved through proliferation. A line from **La Forza del Destino** will illustrate. Don Carlo wrongly thinks that Don Alvaro has deliberately killed Don Carlo's father and seduced his sister. In vain Carlo pursues Alvaro all over Spain and Italy, only to finally meet up with him (by which time Alvaro has become a monk and a hermit!) at the entrance to his hermit's cave-retreat. When Carlo challenges Alvaro to a duel, the latter meekly asks only to be left alone. Alvaro shows supreme self-control, not even reacting to Carlo's bigotted taunt: "sangue tinto di mulatto"—tainted Mulatto blood—a degrading reference to Alvaro's half-Incan ancestry. Enraged, Carlo throws these powerful words at Alvaro:

"Non si   placa   il mio   furor'
One doesn't placate my   fury
Con   mendaci   deliri   accenti!"
With mendacious,   delirious 'words'!

"Accenti", "mendaci", "deliri": each of these words is unusual, imaginative and powerful.   Taken together, they have enormous impact. The concision and suggestiveness of such phrases is impressive; their rarity is further evidence that opera does not yield its deepest secrets (and its greatest joys) easily.

The third aspect is poetic devices. A good libretto will abound in these. **Rigoletto** is typical, glistening with highly original metaphors. Reflecting on Sparafucile, the hired assassin whom he has just met in a deserted street, Rigoletto ponders philosophically on the roles which fate forces us to play and the strange, hidden links between seeming opposites:

---

[1] Another excellent example is the Duke in **Rigoletto**. Courting the Countess of Ceprano at the beginning of the play, he sings these irresistible words:
Per voi   già   possente   la fiamma   dell'amore
For you   already powerful   the flame   of love
Inebria,   conquide, distrugge (il) mio cuore!
Inebriates, conquers, destroys   my heart!
Note the energy and the unusual juxtaposition of these three verbs.

Pari	siamo!	Io,	la lingua;	egli ha	il pugnale!
We are the same!		I (have)	the tongue;	he has	the dagger!

L'uomo	son'io che ride;	ei	quel	che	spegne!
The man I am who laughs;		he (is)	the one	who	extinguishes!

As the metaphors suggest, the two men have profound similarities. Rigoletto kills with poisoned words; Sparafucile kills with the dagger. How grotesque yet how original and effective to compare a dagger to a tongue! There's daggers in men's smiles... Note that the verb "ho" has been dropped after "Io" (line 1). This is an elipse.

Another poetic device which is especially suited to the often paradoxical realm of opera is the oxymoron (usually an adjective which clashes with a noun). Butterfly's description of herself as "rinnegata e felice" (renounced/ostracized and happy) is typical and it sums up her situation well. Marriage to Pinkerton ostracizes her yet makes her supremely happy. She uses this phrase "rinnegata e felice" several times, each time with great dramatic power. Doubtless this too is the kind of language which Verdi was referring to in his remarks to Ghislanzoni: "the world (...) that (...) brings the stage situation to life." (see p. 33).

As for good wit, it would be hard to find a better example than the following from **Rigoletto**. The scene is intensely dramatic: the jester has just discovered that his daughter is missing. He suspects the Duke and his courtiers and when he confronts the latter, the following brilliant exchange takes place:

Rigoletto: "La ra, la ra, la ra, la ra, la ra, la ra!

Courtiers: "O buon' giorno, Rigoletto!"

Rigoletto (to himself): "Han' tutti fatto il colpo!
                        (They all did the deed!)

Ceprano (a courtier): "Ch'hai di nuovo, Buffon'?"
                      (What's new, Jester?)

Rigoletto (imitating him sarcastically):
>   "Ch'hai di nuovo,   Buffon'?
>   Ch'hai di nuovo,   Buffon'?!
>
>   Che dell'usato più   noioso voi siete!"
>   That than usual more boring you are!
>   (That you are more boring than usual!)

Such quick, sparkling wit does much to enliven a libretto. Unfortunately, however, wit, puns, etc. are usually lost in translation.

I wrote earlier (p. 1) that Metastasio set the model of language which most librettists were to follow. Although this is true, it should also be remembered that two great literary movements, Romanticism and Realism ("Verismo" in Italian), had considerable impact on the evolution of the libretto. This impact has probably been noticeable from the quotations which I have used in this book. It is evident that the libretto of **La Bohème** contains much more difficult language than the libretto of **Don Giovanni**. From 1787 (**Don Giovanni**) to 1896 (**La Bohème**) opera's vocabulary expanded a lot. Romanticism introduced new, exotic worlds, whether Roman Gaul (**Norma**) or Scotland (**Lucia di Lammermoor**). With these new worlds come new words, or rather, in many cases, old words in a new (operatic) context. A line from **Norma** sums it all up when she warns the Gauls that they are not ready to take on the Roman army:

>   Ancor' non sono della nostra   vendetta
>   Yet   are   not   of   our   vengeance
>
>   I   dì   maturi.
>   The days mature (ready).
>
>   Delle   sicambre   scuri
>   Than the   Sicambrian   axes
>
>   Sono i   pili   romani   ancor' più forti.
>   Are the Roman javelins still   stronger.

"Sicambre scuri" and "pili romani" are ancient, rather esoteric words but they create just the right local color.

135

Later in the 1800's Realism brought into play all kinds of everyday words, often for local color as well. Alfio's description of the joys of the carter's vagabond life in **Cavalleria Rusticana** is typical:

> Il cavallo scalpita,
> The horse stamps,
>
> I sonagli squillano,
> The bridle-bells jingle,
>
> Schiocca la frusta. Ehi là!
> Crack goes the whip. Hey, there! (See photo, p. 31d).

The words are colorful and suggestive, but they are also concrete and specialized. A Sicilian cart has become a subject of interest in itself, which would have been unthinkable in Mozart's very psychological operas. For vocabulary (but not necessarily for ideas—no librettos are deeper than Mozart's—) librettos seem to become increasingly difficult as you move from Mozart to Puccini. Compare the following passages, one from Mozart's **Don Giovanni** (1787), the other from Leoncavallo's **I Pagliacci** (1892). The passages are neatly comparable because in each the character laments the distasteful realities of his station in life.

First, Leporello, who must do the bidding of a callous, selfish, dangerous master:

> Notte e giorno faticar'
> Night and day to labor
>
> Per chi nulla sa gradir';
> For one whom nothing can please;
>
> Pioggia e vento sopportar',
> Rain and wind to endure,
>
> Mangiar' male e mal' dormir'!
> To eat badly and to sleep badly!

136

```
Voglio   far'    il     gentiluomo
I want   to play  the    gentleman

E non voglio   più          servir'!
I don't want   any longer   to serve!
```

The lines are short and the vocabulary limited to the 'classical', i. e. the refined and somewhat abstract language of the court ("faticar'", "gradir'"). This is essentially courtly language designed to please courtly people.

How different is Canio's lament in **I Pagliacci**!

```
Tu    sei    Pagliaccio!
You   are    Pagliaccio!

Vesti   la giubba   e        la      faccia      infarina,
Put on  the jacket  (1)and   (3) (your) face    (2) powder,

La gente   paga   e       rider'       vuole   qua.
People     pay    and to laugh         want    here.

E   se    Arlecchin'   t'invola        Colombina,
And if    Harlequin    steals    (your) Columbine,

Ridi,     Pagliaccio,  e       ognun'     applaudirà!
Laugh,    Pagliaccio,  and     everyone   will applaud!

Tramuta in         lazzi   lo spasimo   ed   il pianto...
Change into merry  pranks  the suffering and the tears...
```

Canio's lines are sinuous and complex. There are specific allusions to characters of the Commedia dell'Arte, like Harlequin and Columbine. Above all, the vocabulary is somewhat specialized and mentions such things as the actor's face powder and the clown's pranks ("lazzi" refers specifically to the Commedia dell'Arte tradition). A century of opera brought a big change.

137

This concludes "Italian for the Opera". I hope that it will help you to understand operatic Italian. It is not an easy subject, but taking the time to study it will enhance immeasurably your appreciation of opera. There really is no other way to understand opera in depth and although innovations like surtitles clarify the gist of what is happening on stage, they are almost always incomplete and, not infrequently, 'out of synch' with the music and the action.

In any case, my book is really only a starter. If you knew little about operatic Italian before reading it, I hope that it has clarified the essentials and put you well on the road to understanding the original. If you already knew a lot of Italian before picking up this book, I hope that it has been of some assistance.

If you wish to delve deeper into libretto Italian, I again recommend William Weaver's "Verdi Librettos" which contains the Italian text on the left hand page and, facing it, a very accurate (and, paradoxically, **highly imaginative**) English translation. If you closely compare the English and the Italian you will soon become confident about the word meanings and the patterns of the original Italian. Read and reread your favorite arias and scenes, preferably listening to them as you do so. (Reading and listening together in this way is a powerful learning device!) Soon you will recognize words and patterns when you encounter them in different contexts. By then you will have opened up to yourself a whole new world of pleasure and understanding. Coraggio e buon' divertimento!

CHAPTER TWELVE

KEYS TO THE EXERCISES

A. EXERCISE ON PP. 22-23.

Al	chiostro	di	San	Giusto
Prep./art.	**noun**	**prep.**		**noun**

Ove	finì	la	vita
Adv.	**verb**	**art.**	**noun**

l'avo	mio	Carlo	quinto,
art./noun	**adj.**	**noun**	**adj.**

stanco	di	gloria	e	onor',
adj.	**prep.**	**noun**	**conj.**	**noun**

la	pace	cerco	invan'
art.	**noun**	**verb**	**adv.**

che	tanto	ambisce	il	cor'.
pron.	**adv.**	**verb**	**art./noun**	

B. EXERCISE ON P. 25.

1. il cantore   masculine
2. il calice   masculine
3. la bellezza   feminine
4. l'ora   feminine
5. la voluttà   feminine
6. il fremito   masculine
7. l'amore   masculine
8. l'occhio   masculine
9. il cuore   masculine
   (core)

C. EXERCISE ON PP. 28-29.

1. Nel	in the		5. Nei	In the	
2. dell'	of the		6. dai	with the	
3. Di	Of		7. Da	From	
4. Ai ai	At the at the				

D. EXERCISE ON PP. 46-48.

1. La   calunnia è   un   venticello,
   art.   noun   verb   art.   noun

2. Un'   auretta assai gentile
   art.   noun   adv. adj.

3. Che   insensibile,   sottile,
   conj. adj.   adj.

4. Leggermente, dolcemente,
   adv.   adv.

5. incomincia,   incomincia a   sussurar'!
   verb   verb   prep. verb

6. Vissi d'arte,   vissi d'amore,
   verb prep.noun   verb prep./noun

7. Non feci mai   male ad   anima   viva!
   **   verb adv.   noun prep. noun   adj.**

8. Con man' furtiva, quante   pene conobbi, allevïai.
   prep. noun adj.   adj.   noun verb   verb

9. Sempre con   'fè   sincera la   mia   preghiera
   adv.   prep. noun adj.   art.   adj. noun

10. ai   santi tabernacoli salì.
    prep./art adj.   noun   verb.

11. Celeste Aïda,   forma   divina,
    adj.   noun   noun   adj.

12. Mistico serto di   luce e   fior',
    adj.   noun prep. noun conj. noun

140

13. Del   mio pensi<u>e</u>ro tu   sei   regina,
prep./art. adj   noun   pron. verb noun

14. Tu   di   mia vita sei   lo   splend<u>o</u>r'.
pron. prep. adj. noun verb art. noun

15. Il   tuo bel ci<u>e</u>lo vorrei ridarti.
art. adj. adj. noun verb verb/pron.

16. Le   dolci brezze del   p<u>a</u>trio su<u>o</u>l'.
art. adj. noun   prep./art. adj.   noun

E. EXERCISE ON P. 59-60.

1. mi: direct object
2. mi: direct object; mi: reflexive
3. ti: dative of advantage
4. ei: subject; Vi: indirect object;   lo: direct object
5. ti: reflexive
6. chi: relative; lei: disjunctive (object of preposition.);
          s': reflexive

F. EXERCISE ON PP. 76-80.

1. vedremo: we will see (future, 1st person plural).
4. appare: appears (present, 3rd person singular).
5. è: is (present, 3rd person singular).
6. entra: enters (present, 3rd person singular).
7. Romba: Booms out (present, 3rd person singular).
8. Vedi?:   Do you see? (present, 2nd person singular).
9. scendo: go down (present, 1st person singular).
10. Mi metto: I put myself (present, 1st person singular).
11. aspetto: I wait (present, 1st person singular).
12. non mi pesa: It doesn't weigh on me
                  (present, 3rd pers. sing.).
14. s'avv<u>i</u>a: makes its way (present, 3rd person singular).
16. sar<u>à</u>:   will (it) be (future, 3rd person singular).
18. dir<u>à</u>:   will he say (future, 3rd person singular).
19. Chiamer<u>à</u>: He will call (future, 3rd person singular).
21. Me ne star<u>ò</u>: I will stay (future, 1st person singular).
24. chiamer<u>à</u>: he will call (future, 3rd person singular).

28. avverrà: will come about (future, 3rd person singular).
29. prometto: I promise (present, lst person singular).
31. l'aspetto: I wait for him (present, lst person).

G. EXERCISES ON PP. 105-107.

1. Go, (my) thought, on golden wings!
2. Go, light upon the slopes and the hills
3. Where the sweet breezes of our birthland
4. Give off a scent tepid and soft.
5. Greet the banks of the Jordan and
6. The ruined towers of Sion.
7. Oh, my fatherland so beautiful and lost!
8. Oh, memory so dear and fatal!
9. Golden harp of the prophetic poets,
10. Why do you hang mute from the willow tree?
11. Kindle memories again in our breast;
12. Tell us of the old days (the time that was).
13. Bring a sound of bitter lament
14. Similar to the fate of Jerusalem.
15. Or may the Lord inspire you with a precept
16. Which might, through our suffering, infuse us with courage!

H. EXERCISE ON PAGES 116-117.

1. If the verb in the first clause is an imperative, a subjunctive sometimes follows (p. 112).
2. If there's a verb of emotion in the first clause, the next clause will be in the subjunctive (p. 113). 'Sia', from essere.
3. The subjunctive always follows certain expressions: benchè, bisogna che, prima che, etc. (p. 113)
4. The present subjunctive form is often used as an imperative. (p. 112).
5. GIUNGA: the subjunctive is required after prima che, etc. p. 113).
   SI RAPISCA: subjunctive used as an imperative (p. 112).
6. The subjunctive is used to convey vagueness, uncertainty, etc. (p. 113). 'Venga' is from 'venire'.

I. EXERCISE ON PAGE 106.

Edgardo:

1. frena (present of **frenare**, to stop, 'put the brake on').
2. troncò (simple past of **troncare**, to cut off).
3. sono (present, 3rd person plural, of **essere**, to be).
4, sta (present of **stare**, to be).
5. sono (present, 1st person singular, of **essere**, to be).
6. amo (present of **amare**).

Enrico:

7. frena (present of **frenare**, to stop, etc.).
8. corse (simple past of **correre**, to run).
9. sorse (simple past of **sorgere**, to rise).
10. è (present of **essere**, to be).
11. ho tradita (compound past of **tradire**, to betray).
12. sta (present of **stare**, to be).
13. posso (present of **potere**, to be able, etc.) plus **spegnere** (to put out, extinguish.).

Lucia:

14. sperai (simple past of **sperare**, to hope).
15. avesse troncato (imperfect subjunctive of **avere** plus the past participle of **troncare**, to cut off. A compound tense: the pluperfect subjunctive. Rather rare. (See page 97).
16. aita (**aiuta** in modern Italian). Present of **aiutare**, to help.
17. vivo (present of **vivere**, to live).
18. cadde (simple past of **cadere**, to fall).
19. tradì (simple past of **tradire**, to betray).
20. vorrei piangere (conditional of **volere**, to wish, plus the infinitive, **piangere**, to cry i. e. to shed tears.)
21. posso (present of **potere**, to be able, etc.).
22. abbandona (present of **abbandonare**).

Notice how the concision of the preterites and the abundance of verbs adds to the forcefulness of this passage.

BIBLIOGRAPHY OF SUGGESTED READINGS AND VIEWINGS.

GENERAL READINGS:

Biancolli, Louis: "The Opera Reader". McGraw-Hill, New York, 1953.

Del Fiorentino, Dante:"Immortal Bohemian: an Intimate Memoir" (on Puccini's life). Prentice-Hall, New York, 1952.

Gatti, Carlo: "Verdi, the Man and his Music". Gollancz, London, 1955.

Hughes, Spike: "Famous Puccini Operas". Robert Hale, London, 1959.

Mordden, Ethan: "Opera Anecdotes". Oxford University Press, New York/Oxford, 1985.

Osborne, Charles: "Letters of Giuseppe Verdi". Gollancz, London, 1971.

Rosenbaum, Peter: "Italian for Educated Guessers: Shortcuts to the language." Forza Press, 1984.

Rosenthal, Harold: "The Opera Bedside Book". Camelot, London, 1965.

Smith, Patrick: "The tenth muse, a Historical Study of the Opera Libretto". Knopf, New York, 1970.

Vickers, Hugh: "Great Opera Disasters". MacMillan, Butler and Tanner; London, 1979.

Weaver, William: "Verdi Librettos". Doubleday, New York, 1963. Very accurate and imaginative translations alongside the original Italian. A "must' for the serious student. Mr. Weaver has also written "Mozart Librettos".

DICTIONARIES:

Collins and Hoare are both highly recommended bilingual dictionaries. The serious enthusiast will find Palazzi or Zingarelli very useful. Both are detailed, comprehensive, and completely in Italian(!).

ON VIDEO:

"LIFE OF VERDI": a superb account of Verdi's life, his loves, his quarrels, his struggles, his music, his relations with his librettists. Produced by Radiotelevisione Italiana. 600 minutes (4 videocassettes) long. Produced in 1983. English, French, and (of course) Italian versions available. Can be ordered from Kultur Video, 121 Hwy 36, West Long Branch, New Jersey, 07764, U.S.A. An excellent **Wagner** with Richard Burton is also available through them.

"PUCCINI": a candid look at Puccini's life, including the tragic suicide of the Puccinis' maid. Wonderful footage of Puccini's house at the lake (Torre del Lago). An excellent mixture of atmosphere reconstruction and realism. Written by Charles Wood, directed by Tony Palmer. Robert Stephens plays the part of Puccini.

"CASANOVA 70": is a hilarious farce about a Swedish woman who visits Italy and, much to the merriment of her Italian hosts, speaks only operatic Italian. With Marcello Mastroianni and Virna Lisi, (1965).

P.S. Mosco Carner's "Puccini: a Critical Biography" is absolutely first rate, easily the best book I have read on Puccini.

INDEX

PHOTO CREDITS

The author wishes to thank the following for their kind permission to embellish this book with their photographs.

p. 31 a, b Photos are from RAI's "Life of Verdi". Kultur Video, 121 Hwy, 36 West Long Branch, New Jersey, 07764, U S A.

p. 31 b **Tosca**. Placido Domingo as Cavaradossi. La Scala, 1974.

p. 31 c **Otello**. Sherrill Milnes as Iago. The Metropolitan Opera, 1972. **Rigoletto**. Louis Quilico (Rigoletto), Maria Pellegrini (Gilda) Canadian Opera Company (Toronto), 1969.

p. 31 d **Cavalleria Rusticana**. Frank Guarrera as Alfio. The Met, 1970. (Photo: Gary Renaud; taken from "Magificence Onstage at the Met", by Robert Jacopson. Verdi's funeral procession in Milan. Museo Teatrale alla Scala.

p. 49 **Il Barbiere di Siviglia**. Basilio and Bartolo. From "Encyclopedia of the Opera", by Peter Gammond. p. 164.

p. 63 Maria Callas. "The Lyric Opera of Chicago", by Claudia Cassidy.

p. 80 **Madama Butterfly**. Renata Tebaldi with Annamaria Canali. The Lyric Opera of Chicago, 1958.

p. 83 **Rigoletto**. Ettore Bastianini as Rigoletto; Richard Tucker as the Duke. The Lyric Opera of Chicago, 1962.

p. 107 **Nabucco**. Boris Cristoff with Chorus. The Lyric Opera of Chicago, 1963.

150